ACCENTS ON SHAKESPEARE

General editor: TERENCE HAWKES

Shakespeare and Feminist Performance

In this controversial new book, Sarah Werner argues that the text of a Shakespeare play is only one of the many factors that give a performance its meaning. By focusing on The Royal Shakespeare Company, Werner demonstrates how actor training, company management and gender politics fundamentally affect both how a production is created and the interpretations it can suggest. Werner particularly concentrates on:

- the influential training methods of Cicely Berry and Patsy Rodenburg
- the history of the RSC Women's Group
- Gale Edwards' production of *The Taming of the Shrew*.

She reveals that no performance of Shakespeare is able to bring the plays to life or to realise the playwright's intentions without shaping them to mirror our own assumptions.

By examining the ideological implications of performance practices, this book will help all interested in Shakespeare's plays to explore what it means to study them in performance.

Sarah Werner received her PhD from the University of Pennsylvania, and has taught in the English and Theatre departments at Penn, McGill, George Washington and George Mason Universities.

ACCENTS ON SHAKESPEARE
General Editor: TERENCE HAWKES

It is more than twenty years since the New Accents series helped to establish "theory" as a fundamental and continuing feature of the study of literature at undergraduate level. Since then, the need for short, powerful "cutting edge" accounts of and comments on new developments has increased sharply. In the case of Shakespeare, books with this sort of focus have not been readily available. **Accents on Shakespeare** aims to supply them.

Accents on Shakespeare volumes will either "apply" theory, or broaden and adapt it in order to connect with concrete teaching concerns. In the process, they will also reflect and engage with the major developments in Shakespeare studies of the last ten years.

The series will lead as well as follow. In pursuit of this goal it will be a two-tiered series. In addition to affordable, "adoptable" titles aimed at modular undergraduate courses, it will include a number of research-based books. Spirited and committed, these second-tier volumes advocate radical change rather than stolidly reinforcing the status quo.

IN THE SAME SERIES

Shakespeare and Appropriation
Edited by Christy Desmet and Robert Sawyer

Shakespeare Without Women
Dympna Callaghan

Philosophical Shakespeares
Edited by John J. Joughin

Shakespeare and Modernity: Early Modern to Millennium
Edited by Hugh Grady

Marxist Shakespeares
Edited by Jean E. Howard and Scott Cutler Shershow

Shakespeare in Psychoanalysis
Philip Armstrong

Shakespeare and Modern Theatre: The Performance of Modernity
Edited by Michael Bristol and Kathleen McLuskie

Shakespeare and Feminist Performance

Ideology on stage

SARAH WERNER

Routledge
Taylor & Francis Group

LONDON AND NEW YORK

First published 2001
by Routledge
2 Park Square, Milton Park,
Abingdon, Oxon OX14 4RN

Simultaneously published in
the USA and Canada
by Routledge
711 Third Avenue,
New York, NY 10017

Routledge is an imprint of the
Taylor & Francis Group

Typeset in Baskerville by
RefineCatch Limited, Bungay, Suffolk

British Library Cataloguing in
Publication Data

A catalogue record for this book is available
from the British Library

Library of Congress Cataloging in
Publication Data

Werner, Sarah,
    Shakespeare and feminist performance :
    ideology on stage / Sarah Werner.
        p.   cm. – (Accents on Shakespeare)
    Includes bibliographical references (p.   ) and
    index.
    1. Shakespeare, William, 1564–1616 –
Stage history – England.   2. Shakespeare,
William, 1564–1616 – Stage history –
1950–   3. Women in the theater – England –
History – 20th century.   4. Feminism and
theater – England – History – 20th
century.   5. Shakespeare, William, 1564–
1616 – Dramatic production.   6. Shakespeare,
William, 1564–1616 – Characters –
Women.   7. Royal Shakespeare Company.
8. Rodenburg, Patsy, 1953– 9. Berry,
Cicely.   10. Edwards, Gale.   I. Title.
II. Series.
    PR3106 .W47   2001
    822.3'3 – dc21   2001018088

ISBN 978–0–415–22729–2 (hbk)
ISBN 978–0–415–22730–8 (pbk)

For Rukesh Korde

Contents

General editor's preface

In our century, the field of literary studies has rarely been a settled, tranquil place. Indeed, for over two decades, the clash of opposed theories, prejudices and points of view has made it more of a battle-field. Echoing across its most beleaguered terrain, the student's weary complaint, "Why can't I just pick up Shakespeare's plays and read them?" seems to demand a sympathetic response.

Nevertheless, we know that modern spectacles will always impose their own particular characteristics on the vision of those who unthinkingly don them. This must mean, at the very least, that an apparently simple confrontation with, or pious contemplation of, the text of a 400-year-old play can scarcely supply the grounding for an adequate response to its complex demands. For this reason, a transfer of emphasis from "text" towards "context" has increasingly been the concern of critics and scholars since the Second World War: a tendency that has perhaps reached its climax in more recent movements such as "New Historicism" or "Cultural Materialism".

A consideration of the conditions – social, political or economic – within which the play came to exist, from which it derives, and to which it speaks will certainly make legitimate demands on the attention of any well-prepared student nowadays. Of course, the serious pursuit of those interests will also inevitably start to undermine ancient and inherited prejudices, such as the supposed distinction between "foreground" and "background" in literary studies. And even the slightest awareness of the pressures of gender or of race, or the most cursory glance at the role played by that strange creature "Shakespeare" in our cultural politics, will reinforce a similar turn towards questions that sometimes appear scandalously "non-literary." It seems clear that very different and unsettling notions of the ways in which literature might be addressed can hardly be avoided. The worrying truth is that nobody can just pick up Shakespeare's plays and read them. Perhaps – even more worrying – they never could.

The aim of *Accents on Shakespeare* is to encourage students and teachers to explore the implications of this situation by means of an engagement with the major developments in Shakespeare studies of the last ten years. It will offer a continuing and challenging reflection on those ideas through a series of multi- and single-author books which will also supply the basis for adapting or augmenting them in the light of changing concerns.

Accents on Shakespeare intends to lead as well as follow. In pursuit of this goal, the series will operate on more than one level. In addition to titles aimed at modular undergraduate courses, it will include a number of books embodying polemical, strongly argued cases aimed at expanding the horizons of a specific aspect of the subject and at challenging the preconceptions on which it is based. These volumes will not be learned "monographs" in any traditional sense. They will, it is hoped, offer a platform for the work of the liveliest younger scholars and teachers at their most outspoken and provocative. Committed and contentious, they will be reporting from the forefront of current critical activity and will have something new to say. The fact that each book in the series promises a Shakespeare inflected in terms of a specific urgency should ensure that, in the present as in the recent past, the accent will be on change.

Terence Hawkes

Acknowledgments

This book has been evolving over a good number of years and there are many people who have helped along the way. The project began at the University of Pennsylvania, and the English Department and its Penn-in-London Program provided invaluable support, particularly for the crucial time I spent living in London. A great debt of thanks is also owed to the Shakespeare in Performance Research Group at McGill University, which gave me a postdoctoral research fellowship that provided both financial support and intellectual stimulus. A number of libraries have been crucial in pulling this together, including the Furness Shakespeare Library at Penn, the Shakespeare Centre Library in Stratford-upon-Avon and the Folger Shakespeare Library in Washington D.C.; the librarians at the Shakespeare Centre in particular helped me to dig up resources that became central to my research, while the Folger staff, in addition to their expertise, made the library a wonderful home while I finished my work.

Both inside and outside of these institutions, many people have helped me through this work. Phyllis Rackin, Cary Mazer and Barbara Hodgdon are owed my first debt of thanks; I hope they see how much of their wisdom has passed onto these pages and that they forgive me for the moments when I chose to overlook their good sense and follow my own stubborn path. Lizbeth Goodman also deserves special mention for her generosity in sharing her research on the Women's Group, her expertise in researching feminist theatre and her immense good will. The many others whose talents and warmth have helped this book along are Mike Bristol, Rebecca Bushnell, Anne Button, Juliet Dusinberre, Will Fisher, Allen Grove, Carolyn Jacobson, Christa Jansohn, Leonore Lieblein, Kristin Lucas, Gordon McMullan, Fiona McNeill, Rose Malague, Michael Newton, Peter Parolin, Ed Pechter, Kristin Poole, Kate Shaw, Jessica Slights and Emily Westmore. My students at Penn and McGill were more helpful than they realized in clarifying my thoughts, and seminar members at the Shakespeare Association of America meetings were no less marvelous at helping me clarify my work. I am particularly indebted to Jane Boston, Terry Hands, Genista McIntosh, Cary Mazer, Fiona Shaw and Susan Lily Todd for making themselves available for interviews. Thanks are also due to Photofest, the Shakespeare Center Library and Cary Mazer for supplying the illustrations. Finally, my editors have been wonderful and patient; my deep thanks to Terry Hawkes for his insight and encouragement, to Talia Rodgers at Routledge and to Rosie Waters for her help in procuring permissions.

Above all, there is my family to thank. Although I would normally be embarrassed to offer such a public tribute to my cat, and he is not even aware of such inclusion, on the off chance that he is much smarter than I give him credit for, I must acknowledge how very much Isaac has helped me in the writing of this book. Even without being able to read, he knows that he is the ruler of our household, and I am sure he is looking forward to not having to share my lap with the computer. My family has been everything and more from the time I first began. For their love and support they each deserve a round of applause: Arnold Werner, Elizabeth Werner, Rachel Werner and Andrew Siderowf. My nephew Ben is too small to have played much of a part in this, but I know he would like being clapped for, so this is his tribute. My partner, on the other hand, deserves much more than a round of applause. Without him I would not be able to be a kept woman or a happy one and, as just a very small token of my love, it is to him that this book is dedicated. Although he might not have been very involved in the creation of this project, he knows that our next and better project is only just around the corner.

An earlier version of the first chapter was published in *New Theatre Quarterly*, and a previous version of the second chapter will also be published in *Shakespeare and Modern Theatre* (Routledge 2001).

Introduction
Local habitations

If we want to look for evidence of Shakespeare's popularity, the end of the twentieth century in America provides ample material. *Shakespeare in Love* was one of 1998's most popular films, earning general acclaim, high ticket sales, thirteen Oscar nominations and several Oscar wins, including Best Picture and Best Actress. Harold Bloom's *Shakespeare and the Invention of the Human* sold an astonishingly high number of copies for a 745-page nonfiction, non-self-help book, appearing in the *New York Times* bestseller list for six weeks. Bloom himself appeared on national television and radio shows to talk about Shakespeare and even, in *Newsweek*, to talk about *Shakespeare in Love*. Newspapers regularly published articles and editorials celebrating Shakespeare's resurgence. And screen Shakespeares continued to accrue. Released in 1999 were *10 Things I Hate About You* (an adaptation of *The Taming of the Shrew* set in high school) and star-studded versions of *A Midsummer Night's Dream* and *Titus Andronicus*; the following year brought *Romeo Must Die* (a martial arts *Romeo and Juliet*), *Hamlet* set in corporate America and a musical verison of *Love's Labours Lost*.

What does all this mean? Is Shakespeare the new hip thing in popular culture? Is his high profile evidence of his continuing timeless appeal? Verlyn Klinkenborg, in an editorial for the *New York Times*, describes this current boom in popular Shakespeare as a fireside conversation we're having about ourselves:

We are watching, in this momentary popular focus on Shakespeare, one of the things that makes Shakespeare fascinating. It's as though at this instant we were huddled around a Shakespearean fire on a night not as harsh as Lear's, of course, but not as magical as Bottom's either. The subject of conversation, as Mr. Bloom makes clear, isn't just Shakespeare. The subject is also all the conversations he has inspired over time. Many men and women, moved by what this one man wrote, have been drawn to this fire, and their voices, of considerable magnitude in themselves, still hover invisibly in the air, like Ariel's or Puck's. The society of readers gathered around this fire is an open one, and it is precisely as broad as the society of Shakespeare's characters. That is to say it includes not only everyone but also, to borrow Mr. Bloom's native hyperbole, everyone possible.

(Klinkenborg 1999: A14)

Our open and broad society, from this account, derives from Shakespeare himself, and his plays allow us to discover our possibilities. But Klinkenborg's fireside conversation is also the antithesis of the academic Shakespeare which attempts "to nullify, by moralizing and historicizing, the deeply human presences we feel in so many of Shakespeare's plays" (Klinkenborg 1999: A14). These omnipresent fireside stories, then, are tales of a very specific sort – stories that Klinkenborg identifies as in the tradition of Samuel Johnson, Charles Lamb, William Hazlitt, G. K. Chesterton and, of course, Bloom himself, stories that "are distinguished by the generosity of their literary insight" (Klinkenborg 1999: A14). It turns out that this is not an open and broad society, but one made up by those who share a very specific viewpoint.

There should be no doubt that Shakespeare's plays do not espouse universal values. In fact, over the centuries they have been appropriated and deployed across the political spectrum to convey specific ideologies in pursuit of particular goals.[1] For all of this, popular belief, like Klinkenborg's editorial, still figures him as our common ground. No matter how many forms he and his plays have taken over the centuries and across the globe, for Anglo-American populations in particular, Shakespeare appears as the founder of our culture and the carrier of our civilization. When John Major's Tory government wanted to install a tougher school curriculum in Britain, they turned to Shakespeare, requiring every 14-year-old to take an examination on one of three set plays (*Julius Caesar*, *Romeo and Juliet* and *A Midsummer Night's Dream*). When the newly organized right-wing National Alumni

Forum in the United States wanted to introduce themselves with a big splash, they turned to Shakespeare as well, claiming in *The Shakespeare File* that the American higher education system was abandoning his plays. Both of these developments turned into significant scandals in their own countries; in each case the media launched ongoing public debates about what political purposes Shakespeare could serve.[2] These discussions were not sparked by actual texts so much as by beliefs about how Shakespeare fits into our lives. In recent years, public discourse about the plays responds not only to their feared absence from the classroom but to their presence in movie theatres. Suggestions that Shakespeare is no longer crucial to our world are met with cries of horror; on the other hand, Shakespeare's colonization of Hollywood is seen as cause for celebration, proof that he is a valuable member of society and that we too, in our appreciation of the Bard, are worthwhile citizens.

From the passion evident in these discussions, Shakespeare clearly remains an important part of our lives. But while these debates can reveal how Shakespeare is deployed across the political spectrum, they also offer a chance to interrogate the mode of his entry into our world. The question of how Shakespeare becomes part of our lives is fundamentally related to the question of what he does for us once he is there – the manner of his entrance affects the role he plays in our debates. Once we start to look at Shakespeare's presence in today's world, it becomes clear that we know him through the performance of his plays, whether on film, on stage or in the classroom. In the last decade, there have been twenty-seven American or British films either of Shakespeare's plays, of adaptations of the plays or about Shakespeare himself.[3] There are 130 Shakespeare theatres or festivals in the United States alone (Londré 1999: 435). And while, contrary to fears, Shakespeare is still taught in schools and universities, students increasingly work with the plays through performance, whether that be by watching staged or filmed productions, by putting on productions of their own or by engaging in informal acting workshops. Books like the Folger Shakespeare Library's series *Set Shakespeare Free* and the Modern Language Association's Options for Teaching volume, *Teaching Shakespeare through Performance*, emphasize performance as the best means for teaching and studying the plays.

What does this prevalence of performed Shakespeare, as opposed to read Shakespeare, mean for the playwright and his plays? For proponents of what J. L. Styan (1977) called the "Shakespeare revolution," the study and experience of Shakespeare on stage leads to a better understanding of the plays; the meaning embedded in the text can come to life and reach out and touch us. But performance does not simply reveal Shakespeare or bring him to life. Whether on stage or on film, it interprets and shapes the plays according to the demands and conditions of the medium. In making the shift from Shakespeare as text to Shakespeare as playscript, we need to study the systems of meaning that constitute performance. Factors such as the *mise-en-scène*, sound design, theatre architecture and acting methods, to name just a few of the elements that contribute to a production's meaning, tend to get left out of the analysis. Too often performances of the plays are discussed only in terms of the text, failing to recognize that it is just one of many factors that determine the meanings we find when watching Shakespeare. The absence of a more comprehensive understanding of performance limits our interpretations of the plays and the uses we make of them.

Consider the advice given in one of the many articles about the teaching of Shakespeare, Linda Kissler's lesson plan for *Henry V*. Kissler's strategy is to use scenes from Kenneth Branagh's and Laurence Olivier's films as illustrations of the text, warning her fellow teachers, "NEVER view any film in its entirety, unless you do so at the end of a unit as a special event" (Kissler 1997: 202). Although she does not explain the rationale for this admonition, her fear might be that watching a film will make reading the play redundant. Kissler frequently relies on the movies as unproblematic realizations of the play's words, beginning her lessons with Branagh's depiction of the siege of Harfleur in order to illustrate what a breach is and to "[get] Shakespeare's words (thanks to Branagh's impeccable diction) ringing in their ears" (Kissler 1997: 202). For the next lesson, she recommends showing the opening of Olivier's film as an introduction to Renaissance theatre history. These films, as she initially explains them, exist solely as illustrations of the play. As the lessons progress, the films serve as aids in interpreting the play. Addressing the issue of students' potential unfamiliarity with the characters from the *Henry IV* plays, Kissler suggests using the flashback scenes from Branagh's film to introduce the characters and issues those plays raise:

> Show your students the tavern scene from Branagh's *Henry V*. You will strengthen the sense of Henry's metamorphosis; you may also want to read them a few lines from Hal's initial soliloquy in *1 Henry IV*. He tells us that when the time is right, he will be a good king. Remind them of Henry's charge to the breach; has he not fulfilled

his promise? Some students will inevitably feel sorry for Falstaff; you
must remind them of Henry's position as monarch. Where could
Falstaff possibly fit in? Talk about friendship. Was Hal ever really
Falstaff's friend? Assure them that while it may be sad – especially in
Branagh's film – Henry really cannot have his former cronies as
friends once he becomes the king. Do you see Henry in a slightly
different way now? What are the qualities that a king should have?
Does Henry have these qualities?

(Kissler 1997: 203–4)

This is not, as Kissler claims, a simple introduction to or familiarization
with ideas – it's an indoctrination into a particular way of reading a
scene. In her interpretation, Henry is the perfect king, emerged from
a troubled adolescence to assume the mantle of responsible adulthood.
While this may be a tempting interpretation when faced with a group
of teenagers and their always potentially disruptive energies (they too
will grow up to be good citizens if taught to emulate Henry, not
Falstaff), it is not the only way in which Shakespeare's or Branagh's
Henry can be viewed.

For a sense of the different ways in which one could look at this
scene, compare Kissler's way of reading with Chris Fitter's more
skeptical take on Branagh's political agenda. Rather than seeing the
flashback to Falstaff as a natural illustration of the King's moral fitness
and emotional growth, Fitter specifies the choices that Branagh made
in filming the scene, and their consequences:

[Falstaff] greets an entering Hal roaringly, and at once asks him not
to banish plump Jack. The scene, however, elevates rather than sub-
verts the Branagh Henry. Falstaff is hard and cold-eyed, witty but
menacing. Henry's "I know thee not, old man" is given only in
voiceover, thought but not stated by a Hal dewy-eyed, grieving.
Henry has thus an aching interiority opened up in him for us, begins
a journey of sensitive, lonely inwardness. Far from being the royal
machiavel, or relishing his status as "maker of manners," he is here
the silent sufferer, victim not origin of necessity.

(Fitter 1991: 268)

Branagh's presentation of this flashback, like that of the other flash-
backs in the film, establishes Henry "as a hero of pious discipline"
(Fitter 1991: 269) rather than as the more complex and ambiguous
figure that Fitter finds in Shakespeare's playscript. Similarly, rather
than understanding the Harfleur sequence as a nice depiction of

French medieval towns and an example of good diction, Fitter reveals the scene as working to set up Branagh's Henry as a hero:

> Henry here delivers the speech in solitude from horseback, his men having fled the breach in panic. It thereby functions as a brilliant trick to win a city apparently lost: through dazzling and solitary oratorical fiction he has won what his soldiers could not.
>
> (Fitter 1991: 268)

Fitter highlights the playscript's moral ambiguities and implicit criticisms of kingship, while Kissler reads Shakespeare's play as one concerning the evolution of a good king; their differing interpretations of the play clearly affect their reactions to Branagh's movie. But Fitter's focus on filmic techniques reveals the problem with Kissler's reliance on the movie as an illustration of the text. Ignoring how Branagh's movie creates its story, Kissler misses the creative nature of filmmaking and her students miss the opportunity to use their critical faculties. Even if she were more attuned to the interpretive process on both the part of director and viewer, her students would not be able to construct an alternate reading of the film. By showing only clips from Branagh's film, Kissler – and any other teacher – ignores the film's use of systematically accumulated meanings. If a teacher were primarily interested in the film's relationship to Shakespeare's playscript, students could do a better job of making sense of the textual omissions and changes were they to see the full pattern of alterations to the script's criticisms of the King.

But it surely also matters how Branagh chooses to present Henry. Individual scenes might not make this apparent, but undoubtedly some students – and many of today's students are adept interpreters of films – would notice the visual parallels between Branagh's film and recent movies about Vietnam.[4] These parallels are a fundamental part of the film's system of meaning; discussing what Branagh does to Shakespeare without discussing what Branagh has done to the genre of Vietnam movies or what the experience of the Vietnam War has done to American culture misses what Branagh's *Henry V* is about. And not to take advantage of students' ability to be keen readers of the visual means a missed chance for them to use those skills to develop their textual acuity.

In this instance, not acknowledging the degree to which non-Shakespearean elements determine the structure and meaning of Branagh's film distorts both the film and the playscript. It also erases the complexities of what performance can offer. By removing the movies from their cultural moments – indeed, by removing the movies even from themselves – teachers make the films into nothing more than fodder for the classroom, tools that exist solely to illustrate textual themes and to help students pass their exams. If these films work only in terms of the playscripts, it is hard to imagine what students make of the films in the cinema, or what would draw them there in the first place. And students do go to see Shakespeare movies in the theatre, even when it is not an assignment and even when they have not read the play. When Baz Luhrmann's *William Shakespeare's Romeo + Juliet* was released, stories circulated of teens and preteens who went to the movie not knowing that the title characters died at the end. Often times those spreading the accounts were horror-struck: how could children today not know the story of Romeo and Juliet? But this rumored ignorance points to a more interesting phenomenon. It wasn't Shakespeare drawing these audiences to theatres, but Leonardo di Caprio and Claire Danes.[5] Hollywood is banking on the fact that adults will go to see *Titus* and kids will go to see *10 Things I Hate About You* based on the appeal of their starring actors, and not because audiences are inherently interested in how those films compare to the playscripts of *Titus Andronicus* and *The Taming of the Shrew*.

Richard Burt's analysis of a moment from *Clueless* (a popular teen adaptation of Jane Austen's *Emma*) reveals the way in which audiences can experience such films through the fun of movie-going rather than as realizations of Shakespeare. At a crucial moment in the trajectory of *Clueless*'s love story, the heroine of the film is able to win the day (or at least the moment) by correctly identifying the speaker of a line from *Hamlet*. When her ex-stepbrother's nerdy girlfriend asserts that Hamlet is the speaker of "To thine own self be true," Cher disagrees. The girlfriend smugly informs her, "I think that I remember *Hamlet* accurately." But Cher's comeback turns out to be devastatingly on target: "Well, I remember Mel Gibson accurately and he didn't say that. That Polonius guy did." Burt reads this scene through the valences of coolness: "the extra-academic Shakespeare can trump the academic one because it is cooler" (Burt 1998: 8). And Cher certainly is cooler than the smug college girlfriend and better able to impress her ex-stepbrother. It's not the fact that Cher knows her Shakespeare through Mel Gibson that is significant – as Burt notes, she is "possibly able to do a cultural critique of *Hamlet* but [is] too cool, too easily bored, actually to bother to do so" (Burt 1998: 9) – but that she knows her Mel Gibson. Aside from Cher's "cool loser" status, what is striking in this moment is the degree to which Gibson has replaced Shakespeare: Gibson becomes the author of *Hamlet*, not our all-important playwright. And if Cher is not interested in performing a cultural critique, it is none the less true that an important aspect of Franco Zeffirelli's film of *Hamlet* is the *Lethal Weapon* series, in which Gibson plays one of the heroes, a similarly frenetic wild man on the verge of madness and suicide. In this way, as Cher knows, it really is Mel Gibson's *Hamlet*, not Zeffirelli's or Shakespeare's.

Hollywood is hardly a reflection of real life, but this moment in *Clueless* depends on what we should already suspect and what the history of Shakespeare in film reflects: that people go to the movies because they like going to the movies and that sometimes Mel Gibson is the author of *Hamlet*.[6] Rather than understanding Shakespeare as a figure of universal interest and performance as a revelation of text, this view recognizes that the performance of Shakespeare serves different purposes for different people. For Cher, learning Shakespeare was an accidental by-product of watching Mel Gibson. For Gibson, performing Shakespeare was a way of moving from action hero to movie hero, increasing both the range of roles available to him and the salary he can command (Hodgdon 1994: 288). This plethora of Shakespeares, Hamlets and Gibsons reveals what classroom videos do not: that the plays are made up of more than words in a text and mean more than the text might attest to.

The recent glut of Shakespeare in American culture, and the general media reaction to it, suggests that the prevailing desire to understand his works as a source of universal and timeless wisdom overlooks the more interesting lesson about how popular culture has currently chosen to focus on the Bard. The success of *Shakespeare in Love* was typically understood in the media as a benchmark of the playwright's own success in and aptness for America. The *New York Times* was particularly swept up in Shakespeare fever in the period between the film's release and its Oscar victories, repeatedly praising his relevancy to our lives. Verlyn Klinkenborg's editorial about our fireside chat (1999) was written in response to the concurrent popularity of the film and Harold Bloom's *Shakespeare: The Invention of the Human*. Michiko Kakutani, the newspaper's book reviewer, wrote an article hailing Shakespeare's modernity and his aptness for our times (Kakutani 1999). Stephen Greenblatt wrote an op-ed piece about the film, the young man of the sonnets and his own minor role in the film's creation. The article, which was featured prominently above other more typically political pieces, pointed out that "Shall I Compare Thee to a Summer's Day?" was more likely to have been written to a ravishing young man than a ravishing young woman and asserted that Greenblatt had suggested to Marc Norman (one of the film's screenwriters) the idea of a film in which Shakespeare has a torrid affair with Christopher Marlowe. Norman didn't pursue the suggestion, to Greenblatt's disappointment, but

> Never mind. "Shakespeare in Love" captured something that all Americans can celebrate: not political cunning, not religious zealotry, not complex moral intelligence, not even love, but supreme, overpowering skill. Our culture adores those who can jump higher, run faster, hit balls farther than anyone else, and our popular artists have invented compelling myths of metamorphosis, tales that recount the transformation of people of modest talents into towering heroes.
>
> (Greenblatt 1999: A15)

The editorial and arts pages of the paper were not alone in touting Shakespeare as an American hero. Even the Circuits section, which focuses on computer technology, praised the film for offering important lessons to today's computer-obsessed youth:

> As 'Shakespeare in Love' reminds us, our cultural heritage comes down to us from men and women who needed no machines to think with, but only the resources of their own naked minds working upon deeply pondered experience – and beyond that, perhaps a sharpened feather to scrawl those thoughts on any writing surface.
>
> (Roszak 1999: G8).

Despite all of this, it would be a mistake to see *Shakespeare in Love* as simply a reflection of Shakespeare's aptness for America. The various public discourses surrounding the film suggest a misleading tautology: we love Shakespeare, so we love *Shakespeare in Love*; and we love *Shakespeare in Love*, so we love Shakespeare. We need to recognize that the film is driven by a much more common Hollywood story: boy meets girl, boy gets girl, boy loses girl. In the process of turning Shakespeare's biography into this love story, the film closed off other avenues of exploration and limited the potential interpretations of his plays. The controversy over *Shakespeare in Love*'s Oscar success revealed some of the categories that shaped the film's reception. Speculation had pitted John Madden's *Shakespeare in Love* against Steven Spielberg's *Saving Private Ryan* as favorites for the top awards. After Spielberg's Oscar for Best Director, the win for *Shakespeare in Love* as Best Picture took many by surprise, including the head of its distributing company:

"I was stunned that 'Shakespeare in Love' won after the Spielberg award," said Joe Roth, chairman of Disney Studios. "It seemed like 'Private Ryan' had all the criteria to take best picture. Why didn't it? Perhaps 'Shakespeare' was able to convince a lot of women voters to vote for it."

(Weinraub 1999)[7]

The suggestion that *Shakespeare in Love* was a woman's film is one that many Oscar watchers would probably have made. The selections for Best Picture that year were particularly – and oddly – bifurcated: Spielberg's *Saving Private Ryan*, a World War II story that contained no significant or even minor speaking female roles; Terrence Malik's *The Thin Red Line*, another World War II story that was populated almost entirely by male actors; Roberto Benigni's *Life is Beautiful*, an Italian comedy about the Holocaust and the relationship between a father and his son; Shekhar Kapur's *Elizabeth*, a historical romance about Queen Elizabeth I's early years on the throne; and Madden's *Shakespeare in Love*. At first glance, the films seem to line up along a split between a masculine World War II and a feminine Renaissance. But *The Thin Red Line*'s complex and skeptical examination of men, heroism and war did as much as *Shakespeare in Love* to counter *Saving Private Ryan*'s simplistic glorification of soldiers and masculinity. And *Elizabeth*'s depiction of political intrigue and femininity was never described as appealing primarily to women.[8]

The further question of why it being a woman's film would help *Shakespeare in Love* is more complicated than Roth's remark allows. Were there more women voting than men? Was the men's block split among the war films? Long before the Oscar ballots were cast, *New York Times* columnist Frank Rich presciently wrote an op-ed piece about the possible defeat of *Saving Private Ryan* by *Shakespeare in Love*. Rich predicted that *Shakespeare in Love* would win because it replicated President Clinton's own triumphs:

> Draft-dodging Bill Clinton beats World War II hero Bob Dole at the polls. Philandering Bill Clinton vanquishes Republican Puritans in the Senate. . . . The nonpartisan, sex-life-and-art-affirming "Shakespeare in Love" arrived at just the right moment to capture "Private Ryan's" fallen flag and take us about as far away from that soiled Washington as a movie possibly can.

(Rich 1999: A19)

Rich's assessment of America's longing to get away from politics was stated more baldly by Stuart Klawans, who noted of the best picture nominees that "their most remarkable feature is a determination to keep their eyes shut tight against present-day American realities" (Klawans 1999a). The tightly shut eyes and sex-life-and-art affirmation of *Shakespeare in Love* clarifies why it could be classified as a woman's picture and *Elizabeth* could not: if *Elizabeth* is a film about the impossibility of mixing love and politics – Elizabeth is betrayed by her lover and threatened with dethronement until she adopts the white-faced virgin image that we are familiar with today – *Shakespeare in Love* is about love leading to success in poetry and business. Shakespeare begins the film in a state of writer's block and sexual impotence: "It's like my quill has broken," he confesses to his therapist. "As if the organ of my imagination is dried up. As if the proud tower of my genius is collapsed. Nothing comes." But with the love of a good woman, Shakespeare not only writes a hit play, he wins the respect of Queen Elizabeth and earns the money to become a shareholder in Richard Burbage's theatre company, which gives him the means to become a gentleman. In *Shakespeare in Love*, romance cures all woes. Describing the film as appealing to women is a short-hand (and sexist) way of describing the film as an apolitical escapist fantasy.

The film's structure and appeal as a love story profoundly affects its depiction of Shakespeare. It seems to suggest that his success comes from his great skill as a writer. His poetry wins over both Viola de Lesseps, who falls in love with him on the basis of his sonnets and plays, and Queen Elizabeth, who judges in his favor a wager with Lord Wessex on the question of whether a play can "show us the very truth and nature of love." The fifty pounds that Wessex must subsequently pay is, we know, the exact sum needed for Shakespeare to become a shareholder in Burbage's company. But while Shakespeare's writing skills lead to his worldly achievements, that capacity to write is founded on his ability to love. The key question for his career – "Can a play show us the very truth and nature of love?" – can be answered only by knowing what love is. Not only does Shakespeare know what love is, he uses his own story as a lover to win the bet. *Romeo and Juliet*, the play that successfully answers Elizabeth's question, is here a thinly disguised account of his and Viola's impossible affair. Key moments in the play are taken from real-life experiences: climbing the balcony to visit a new lover, waking up in the morning to wish that it was still night, the betrothal of your love to another. Other aspects of the play are clearly metaphors for their romance: the lovers' deaths at the end, while not literally the deaths of Shakespeare and Viola, are the metaphorical result of the impossibility of their desired union. Importantly, the performance Elizabeth witnesses is one that stars Shakespeare and Viola as Romeo and Juliet. Acting the play in the brief moment between Viola's marriage and her departure for Virginia, Shakespeare and Viola are playing their own love story for the audience. Elizabeth, who recognizes the truth of their love for each other and their necessary separation, is acknowledging not only a playwright's creation but their real-life love. By making Wessex, who had received the fifty pounds from Viola's father at their betrothal, hand over the wager to Viola, who is then able to pass it on to Shakespeare, Elizabeth both enables Viola to dispose of her own dowry and legitimizes the romance. Shakespeare wins the wager – and his successful career – by being a worthy lover.

The centrality of Shakespeare's talents as a lover, however, is complicated by the way he is gendered in the film. Although the premise of the film and its early trailers resolutely heterosexualize Shakespeare – a cross-dressed Viola joins the acting troupe and they fall in love, obscuring the sexual relations that historically pertained to boy actors and adult males – the way in which their affair is played out allows for more flexibility of gender and sexuality than is usually found in Hollywood films. Viola becomes a part of the cast, not by playing a woman's role, the role one might expect her, as a woman, to take, but by acting the part of a man. Rather than erasing the sexual tensions that could exist between boys and adult men in theatrical troupes, the film allows some of those possibilities to appear briefly in its narrative. It is while Viola is still pretending to be Thomas Kent that she first kisses Shakespeare. Although the audience is under no illusion that this is anything other than a heterosexual kiss, since we know that Thomas Kent is really Viola and Shakespeare is immediately afterward informed of this fact as well, the flirtation and kiss still appear visually as an adult man's attraction to a boy. Subsequent scenes in the film show them kissing, both in front of other actors and in private, with Viola's disguise mustache allowing her to appear in those moments as both male and female. Shakespeare is never clearly depicted as having homosexual or bisexual desires, and it is impossible to read the film as telling anything but an ultimately heterosexual narrative. Even Christopher Marlowe's sexuality is never alluded to, aside from the casting of openly gay actor Rupert Everett. But the repeated scenes of Shakespeare kissing Viola with and without her mustache do destabilize the movie's depiction of heterosexual desire.

Just as desire is destabilized, so are notions of Shakespeare's masculinity. Aside from the obvious initial impotence jokes that deflate his male potency, he repeatedly plays the part of a woman. Most obvious,

Plate 1 Gwyneth Paltrow as Thomas à Kent in *Shakespeare in Love* (dir. John Madden, Miramax, 1999). Photo supplied by Photofest.

perhaps, is when he dresses up as a woman to accompany Viola to meet the Queen. In the scenes at Greenwich, Shakespeare does what he only once depicts in his plays: while a number of his heroines cross-dress as boys, only one man ever dresses in women's clothes. It is possible that the film's depiction of this meeting between Shakespeare and the Queen is a witty allusion to Falstaff's transvestism in *The Merry Wives of Windsor* (written, legend has it, in response to the Queen's desire to see Falstaff in another play), but the scene works most clearly to queer Shakespeare's masculinity. In gown and wimple, he speaks in a falsetto and looks on helplessly in the role of Viola's nurse while she is presented as another man's trophy.

The depiction of Shakespeare as a woman is played out more interestingly in the extended sequence where, in bed with Viola, he speaks Juliet's lines to her. Intercut with scenes of the actors rehearsing, Shakespeare and Viola's lovemaking is also a rehearsal for the play. Shakespeare shows Viola his newest additions to the script while she admires the beauty of the language. Her reading of Romeo's part is soon eclipsed by Shakespeare's reciting of Juliet's lines while they are having sex. There is no mistaking who is speaking whose lines in this scene, even for viewers unfamiliar with the play. "O Romeo, Romeo, wherefore art thou Romeo" (2.1.75), sighs Shakespeare as Viola kisses him; moments later he asks, "What man art thou that, thus bescreened in night, / So stumblest on my counsel?" (2.1.94–5) As the sequence progresses, Shakespeare's naked body is contrasted not only with Juliet's voice, but with Viola's own naked torso, so that Shakespeare's masculinity is never erased. The climax of the scene comes with Shakespeare speaking Juliet's account of the depth of her love: "My bounty is as boundless as the sea, / My love as deep. The more I give to thee, / The more I have, for both are infinite" (2.1.175–7). A naked Shakespeare is on top of an undressed Viola, thrusting his pelvis as he speaks these lines, Viola joining him for the last line's assertion of the infinite. If one juxtaposes this moment with the exaggeratedly Freudian description of Shakespeare's impotence at the start of the film, as we are surely invited to do, one sees an unusual depiction of masculine virility. If Shakespeare initially speaks of towers falling and quills breaking, these lines of the boundless depths of an infinite sea are equally available as an over-the-top quintessentially feminine experience of sexuality. In meeting Viola, Shakespeare has not just recovered his virility, but exceeded it. "Stay but a little; I will come again" (2.1.180) is his line as well as Juliet's. By opening himself to femininity, Shakespeare has regained his masculinity. This is not a moment of gay sexuality, but it is a queering of heteronormative standards, in which men and women are separate, if not always equal, and it offers a decidedly postmodern understanding of the fluidity of gender and sexual identity.[9]

A number of academics who reviewed the film were disappointed that *Shakespeare in Love* depicted Shakespeare as, in the words of one reviewer, so "potently heterosexual" (Cowell 1999). Katherine Duncan-Jones claims, as did Stephen Greenblatt, that "If Shakespeare did fall in love in 1593, surviving documents suggest that it was with a young earl, not a young girl," and complains about the movie's erasure of all non-heterosexual desire:

When he falls in love with the fictitious stage-struck heiress Viola de Lesseps, [there is not] even a bat's squeak of bisexuality. The wispy moustache that is part of her boy's disguise seems to be a wholly effective passion-killer. Even Shakespeare's chum and rival, Kit Marlowe (Rupert Everett), turns out to have been murdered in a quarrel over a 'bill', not a 'lewd love'. The determined exclusion of the Elizabethan theatre's well attested homosociality from such a modern and culturally streetwise film is peculiar.

(Duncan-Jones 1999: 18)

Duncan-Jones proceeds to blame Marc Norman for this omission, defending Stoppard from any such heterosexism.[10] But while these might be reasonable academic responses to the film as a biography of Shakespeare, they miss what the film signifies about Shakespeare to a modern audience. Wanting to see a Shakespeare who is recognizably gay, these viewers miss the Shakespeare whose queer androgyny signals his modernity. His ability to be both male and female sets him apart from most of the other early modern characters in the film, who remain bound to a traditional gender politics of male superiority. Shakespeare's queer masculinity is matched in this by Viola's queer femininity. Viola's desire to act on stage, her refusal to be treated as a piece of property, her successful masquerade as a boy and a stage-hero, all work to make her a modern woman who finds the constraints of Renaissance femininity stifling. It is only by dressing up as a boy that Viola is able to fulfill her desires and woo the man of her dreams, and it is only by dressing as a woman that Shakespeare attains his success. Through their love for each other, both Shakespeare and Viola are able to discover and express their inner selves – the woman within Shakespeare, the man within Viola. Ultimately, Shakespeare is our hero, not just because he is a successful playwright or a successful lover but because he recognizes his inner woman.

While Shakespeare's androgyny modernizes him, it does not make him politically progressive. The focus on Shakespeare as romantic hero removes him from the world of political action and elevates him to a timeless immortality. Never does he make the argument for women's equality outside of the bedroom, never does he make the connection between Viola's enforced marriage to Wessex and the traffic in women that he and Burbage are complicit in with Rosaline. But this political shortcoming is not Shakespeare's alone. The film's story depends on the necessary absence of women from the Renaissance stage as well as the necessary absence of women from the world of public power, but it never places those exclusions within the context of their complex early modern ideology. Viola and Elizabeth are evident exceptions to the norm, but they remain exceptions whose status is never questioned. The one woman who does wield power in the film is unable to use it to alter the system: Elizabeth cannot change the fact that Viola must marry Wessex nor the fact that it is indeed a man's world. Her unwillingness even to try appears a merely personal choice in the absence of a coherent political context. Her decision that Shakespeare and Viola must finally separate is predicated on nothing more than the screenwriters' unwillingness for once to be anachronistic. Although

Norman and Stoppard imaginatively step outside of historical fact when it suits their purpose (Elizabeth goes to a public theatre? Viola goes to a Virginia plantation in 1595? Shakespeare sees a therapist?), here the reliance on historical necessity precludes the possibility of political challenges. *Shakespeare in Love* must adhere to the strictures of the love story, and Viola's earlier transgressions are erased by her ultimately feminine and passive role as muse. In the end, Viola submits to her duty as Wessex's wife, while Shakespeare turns to his art, embarking on the creation of *Twelfth Night* and retelling their love story as a comedy. Dutiful subjects, Shakespeare and Viola go about their lives as they were, sublimating their contrary desires into the roles of artist and muse. With this ending, audiences fulfill their romantic longings through the combination of desire and loss that is so characteristic of Shakespearean drama, but without exploring the more subversive aspects of the plays' unruliness.

Hailed by commentators as evidence of the playwright's enduring appeal, *Shakespeare in Love* is less concerned with the plays than it is with a romantic depiction of their author. That Shakespeare falls in love and writes about his affair becomes evidence both of his own humanity and his plays' universality. But the emphasis on the love story makes this telling of *Romeo and Juliet* a very specific one, removing it from the realm of ideological discourse. Love takes precedence over social upheaval. *Shakespeare in Love*, of course, is not a straightforward performance of *Romeo and Juliet*. Although this film's interpretation of the playscript is looser than those of Baz Luhrmann's *William Shakespeare's Romeo + Juliet* and Franco Zeffirelli's *Romeo and Juliet*, its manipulations are not necessarily more exaggerated. Kenneth Branagh's films of Shakespeare, often cited as successful and traditional examples of the plays on screen, rely on equally specific interpretations and draw on equally local traditions of cinema for their effect.[11] In all of these movies, from deceptively transparent enactments to freer adaptations, the act of filming Shakespeare's plays shapes what meanings are created, giving rise to new meanings that always exceed the words in the playscript. In *Shakespeare in Love*, the filmic conventions of love shape the story that is told while foreclosing possible political readings of the script. In other instances, different extratextual elements will shape the performances. Regardless of specific factors, the process of performing affects what meanings can be attached to the plays. We need to employ a theory of how performances are created in order to examine which interpretations are sidestepped or are made impossible to conceive.

My insistence that the meanings of Shakespeare lie not in his text but in the myriad other aspects that make up a performance might, to dedicated literary scholars, seem perverse. Understanding Shakespeare through the transient elements of performance rather than the (wished-for) solidity of the text is not the method by which most scholars or students approach the plays. But, as will become clear, these apparently transient elements are as crucial in the production of meaning as Shakespeare's words. The move away from a New Critical interpretive practice, in which a text's meaning is understood to be contained solely within the text itself, has led to a wide range of interpretive methods that see meaning located in the web of social relations between individual texts and cultural ideologies. Feminist criticism, new historicism, cultural materialism, queer theory – all insist that meaning does not reside solely within an ahistorical text. In establishing the meaning of Shakespeare through the performance of his plays rather than their status as printed objects, performance criticism has also moved along this trajectory, shifting from a reliance on the text to an examination of the whole creative process. J. L. Styan, who in 1977 called for the institution of performance studies of Shakespeare, was, in James Bulman's phrase, "a card-carrying essentialist" who believed "that Shakespeare's texts are stable and authoritative, that meaning is immanent in them, and that actors and directors are therefore *interpreters* rather than *makers* of meaning" (Bulman 1996: 1; emphases in original). Recent work in Bulman's 1996 anthology, *Shakespeare, Theory, and Performance*, and new books by W. B. Worthen (1997) and Barbara Hodgdon (1998), among others, suggest a different way of working with performances of the plays. Worthen moves away from the text as the locus of Shakespearean meaning, viewing the stage (and stage practices) not as a place where the plays are realized, but rather as an important site for their production and iteration. Similarly skeptical of the claims of literary studies to access the "real" meaning of Shakespeare, Hodgdon's method of analysis "involves opening up a traffic between literary and theatrical cultures that resituates the study of performed Shakespeare within cultural studies," a move that "entails a shift from textual to cultural authority" (Hodgdon 1998: xiii). Both Worthen and Hodgdon argue that performed meaning is something that is created, not found, by directors, actors and audience. In recognizing that the choices theatre practitioners make affect how a play is received, they take us further down the path of understanding how performance works. But performance does not work only through a shift from textual to cultural authority. At the most basic level, each performance is built from a series of specific material and ideological factors: the choice of script, the arena for performance, the hiring or casting of production team and actors, the makeup of the audience which comes to the show. These shape what Shakespeare can mean and how meaning is generated. These are the details we need to understand in order to examine how Shakespeare enters our lives.

To address these issues, I will look specifically at one theatre company's devotion to Shakespeare and the roles that women have in their productions of the plays. The Royal Shakespeare Company conceives of and markets itself as the world's premier performer of Shakespeare. The books and articles that focus on its productions and acting techniques influence not only other theatre companies, but also academic writings about performance and educators' use of performance in the classroom. Its status is particularly seductive because the RSC appears so decidedly neutral – as stated in the 1995 season program,

> The aims of the RSC are in essence much the same today as those expressed by Frank Benson in 1905: 'to train a company, every member of which would be an essential part of a homogeneous whole consecrated to the practice of the dramatic arts and especially to the representation of the plays of Shakespeare.
>
> (Royal Shakespeare Company 1995)

This selfless devotion to Shakespeare might sound harmless initially. What could be wrong with bringing his plays to life? But as subsequent chapters will show, the RSC's practices are built on and create specific ideological readings that limit both the possible meanings of the plays and the role of Shakespeare in our world. By carefully examining actor training at the RSC, the company's corporate structure and the reactions of reviewers to performances, I will argue that no performance of Shakespeare can be understood as neutral. In focusing specifically on one aspect of the company's theatrical practice, that of feminist performance, I am able to explore how the myriad aspects of performance practice collide and overlap in shaping interpretations of Shakespeare. Women's work on the plays as actors and directors has continually been measured by whether or not it lives up to expectations of universality. But, as this book will show, the cultural and ideological practices embedded in the creation and reception of productions need to be interrogated before we can think about the value of such expectations.[12]

In choosing to focus on the Royal Shakespeare Company, I do not mean to suggest that its productions are either more decidedly neutral or more limiting than those of other producers of Shakespeare. But because it is so often held up as the preeminent Shakespeare company, it is easy to miss the ways in which the RSC has made specific, local choices. Many current films of the plays, such as *Shakespeare in Love*, *Titus* or *Hamlet*, are easy to recognize as specific interpretations; not only are they not produced in either of Shakespeare's original media (theatre or print), they are not intended to be uninflected performances of any of his scripts. However, since Shakespeare wrote for the theatre, it is easy to assume that our own theatre can reproduce the sort of experience that he would have intended. This is, of course, Styan's point about the convergence of modern theatrical practice with Shakespeare's own theatrical language; we might not dress in doublet and hose, but our flexible and non-realistic theatre uses the same language that Shakespeare's did, and so can access his intended meanings. The specifics of Styan's argument aside (and it is easy to point out some assumptions that he too readily makes about modern theatre), the stage continues to appear as a false universal. We assume that it is both possible and desirable to capture the essence of Shakespeare in the theatre. However, by looking at how one company strives to capture the real Shakespeare on stage, I will argue that all performances of Shakespeare engage in localized production of meaning.

The first chapter focuses on the type of actor training that is predominant at the RSC. The ongoing influence of Cicely Berry as its voice coach creates an RSC acting style that has come to be the hallmark both of its productions and of Shakespeare performances more generally. The strength of voice work, for its practitioners and for the academics who study it, lies in its ability to give actors a direct and comfortable access to Shakespeare's words, access that they can they use in the service of any production and any interpretation. But in practice and theory, the ways in which voice work teaches actors to read and perform the text depend on specific notions of character and Shakespeare that limit its potential for dissident readings of the plays. For feminist actors, voice work sets up a falsely universal notion of character that relies on a male norm of interpretation, ignoring the problems that character reading has for Shakespeare's female roles. Although voice work relies on maleness as a neutral universal, it operates as a distinctly female practice, taught in private tutorials by women who are subservient to male directors and a male Shakespeare.

The second chapter examines the RSC Women's Group, a little-studied moment of feminist activism within the company that can trace its roots to voice work and to the frustrations involved in creating a sisterhood within the male company. Although the group lasted little more than a year and succeeded in staging only one, non-Shakespearean play (Deborah Levy's *Heresies*), the circumstances surrounding its creation and dissolution reveal some of the ideological factors that shape women's roles in producing Shakespeare. While the frustrations of the original participants found voice in their work on *As You Like It*, very material concerns about money, careers and company organization affected the choices they, and others, were subsequently to make in trying to incorporate women and feminism into the RSC. Always contained within the larger ethos of the company, the Women's Group found its access to Shakespeare limited by economic and ideological preconceptions about the relationship women can have to the plays; although Shakespeare's work is touted as universal, in this instance the gendering of its caretakers clearly illustrates the local nature of its production.

The third chapter proceeds as a case study of Gale Edwards' 1995 RSC production of *The Taming of the Shrew*. Edwards was only the third woman to direct on the main stage in the company's history; faced with a play that was explicitly about gender politics and a company and audience that expected a woman to have a special take on its troubling ideology, Edwards offered a chance to explore the issues about per- formed Shakespeare that I have raised above. The chapter starts with an examination of the playscript and works through the production itself and reactions to it, ending with a consideration of the nature of interpreting performed Shakespeare and the challenges inherent in performance criticism. Having argued for the study of Shakespeare that includes the methods of its enactment, I here consider how to read performance as an examination of local ideologies and material condi- tions. It turns out, unsurprisingly, to be not a straightforward enterprise but one that raises important questions – questions that need to be addressed for the continuation of performance criticism to be valuable.

The Epilogue returns to the relation between text and performance that I have begun to consider here. Turning to an experimental uni- versity production of *Two Gentlemen of Verona*, I use its defamiliarized theatrical language to suggest how all performances rely as much on a theatrical language to shape their meaning as on the textual language of Shakespeare's script. Whereas the RSC describes itself as being "consecrated to his [Shakespeare's] memory" (Noble 2000: 5), Cary Mazer and the actors of the University of Pennsylvania's Theatre Arts production of *Two Gentlemen* are less reverent in their treatment of the playwright, striving to turn Shakespeare upside-down and turning this comedy into a tragedy through its performance.

1

The ideologies of acting and the performance of women

Although the Royal Shakespeare Company prides itself on being consecrated to the representation of Shakespeare, it is not a traditional ensemble whose notion of the plays can easily be identified. Despite Peter Hall's desire to create a coherent, European-style ensemble as he transformed the Shakespeare Memorial Theatre into the Royal Shakespeare Company in the early 1960s, the RSC has never been a company with a unified policy beyond that implied by a vague dedication to Shakespeare. It has certainly never been a company that centered on an ensemble of actors. Although the RSC claims that it "is formed around a core of actors and actresses with the aim that their skills should continue, over the years, to produce a distinctive approach to theatre" (Royal Shakespeare Company 1995), the performers in that core do not remain with the company long enough to produce the "coherence that might define a company of actors, a shared knowledge and experience" (Holland 1997: 22). A study of the cast lists over the years reveals a large number of actors who have stayed at the RSC only for a couple of seasons. Although a core group of directors has remained – indeed the presence of only four artistic directors in almost thirty years suggests some continuity – recent years have seen a growing reliance on outsiders. Without an ensemble of actors, a consistent circle of directors or a clearly articulated company policy, the RSC identity is largely driven by and maintained through the presence of Cicely Berry, its long-time voice coach. As Peter Holland argues, "Berry's status within the company as a cross between coach and first-aider ensured that her principles of work continued to exemplify the RSC style" (1997: 23). This has proved to be the case even when the directors and actors were unfamiliar with or uninterested in the veneration of language that has become the company's hallmark.

Not only has Berry helped to develop a coherent RSC style, she has made that style influential throughout Anglophone theatre. Berry joined the RSC in 1970 as the first full-time voice coach to be associated with a theatre company in Britain and is widely hailed as one of the most influential voice teachers in English-language theatre. Her method of training actors has influenced not only those who have worked at the company in the last thirty years, but those actors and voice teachers she has taught at the Central School for Speech and Drama (an influential institution in the teaching of voice and the only drama school to offer a postgraduate certificate in voice work), those with whom she has worked in prison and school workshops and in private sessions, and those actors, teachers and non-theatre practitioners who have read her books, *Voice and the Actor* (1973) and *The Actor and His Text* (1987). The principles of her work have also spread through the practice of Patsy Rodenburg, a colleague of Berry's at the RSC for nine years, the creator of the voice and text program at the Stratford, Ontario Shakespeare Festival, the founding and current Head of Voice at the Royal National Theatre, Head of Voice at the Guildhall School of Music and Drama, and author of her own successful series of books, *The Right to Speak* (1992), *The Need for Words* (1993) and *The Actor Speaks* (1997). Although there are important differences between their coaching techniques and philosophies, Berry and Rodenburg have fostered ways of working with voice and text that often overlap and are often perceived as teaching aspects of the same method. Between these two women, we can trace an arc of influence that covers Britain's two most prominent theatre companies, two of Britain's most prestigious acting schools and countless numbers of readers and workshop participants throughout Britain, the United States and Canada, as well as numerous other nations worldwide.[1] In order to evaluate performed Shakespeare today, we must first interrogate the method and ideology of voice work.

Over the last twenty-five years, Berry's and Rodenburg's books have served to formalize and disseminate their way of reading and performing the plays, reaching out to all potential readers and unifying us in a desire better to understand Shakespeare and ourselves.[2] Although their access to a wide audience makes these texts influential, they are not completely representative of their authors' training practices; a number of theatre practitioners have commented to me on the books' occasional distance from their authors' studio methods. This distance should not detract from their value as objects of study. If, as Richard Paul Knowles points out in his important examination of voice work, "it may seem unfair to interrogate printed texts written by voice coaches and teachers rather than the methods they employ in their studios and rehearsal halls," it is also true that "*as* texts, these books encode and reinforce ideological structures and assumptions that are both deeply embedded in theatrical discourse and too easily overlooked or mystified when their methods are applied in practice" (Knowles 1996: 93; emphasis in original). Certainly the consistency in each author's body of writings suggests that their written work is not random or accidental, but can serve as a cohesive introduction to their philosophies of voice and acting. The close reading encouraged by voice training can be turned on the trainers' texts themselves to capture those moments of mystification and reveal the social practices that determine the parameters of actors' performances.

While voice and speech training have long histories in the acting community, the current method influencing the RSC stems from Berry's work with Peter Brook on his 1970 *A Midsummer Night's Dream*, which she repeatedly describes as crucial to her development as a voice coach (Parker 1985: 33, Berry 1992: 20 and Berry 1997a: 95–6).[3] The concerns central to theatre practitioners in the late 1960s and early 1970s were also central to the development of Berry's method. Like Brook, Berry believes in the value of empty space (Brook 1968), though for her, that empty neutral arena becomes the body itself: if the "Shakespeare revolution" demonstrated that a literal and metaphorical empty space was necessary to allow Shakespeare to speak for himself (Styan 1977), voice work posits that a similarly empty space needs to be cleared to allow us to find our true voices and speak for ourselves (Knowles 1996: 93–94). Although for academics the importance of voice work usually lies in its readings of the plays, for these voice teachers its importance lies equally in its ability to recover this healthy space that allows our best, natural selves to emerge. Shakespeare is not incidental to this process, and in his role as author he assumes the figure of benevolent guide to our natural selves.

The fundamental connection between voice and self can be found throughout these texts. Your voice, Berry tells us, is not only "the means by which you communicate your inner self" (1973: 12), it *is* your inner self: when you breathe in deeply, "you are touching down to your centre, you are finding the 'I' of your voice" (1973: 22). Rodenburg also takes as a starting-point this belief in the link between voice and self, explaining that our voices reveal "the deepest parts of ourselves" (1992: x) and that work on the voice "can liberate and transform both our use of language and our sense of ourselves" (1993: xv). Those who work with Berry and Rodenburg take this fundamental connection as the root of their praise for the women. Peter Brook's highest tribute to Berry, that "after a voice session with her I have known actors speak not of the voice but of a growth in human relationships" (Berry 1973: 3), is one echoed by later actors and directors: Trevor Nunn's foreword to *The Actor and the Text* (the revised title for the 1992 reprint of *The Actor and His Text*) and Antony Sher's foreword to *The Need for Words* both laud Berry's and Rodenburg's personal warmth and strength as human beings. Ian McKellen's foreword to *The Right to Speak* praises Rodenburg as well, but specifically her strength as a woman and a feminist; he is the only one to comment on the fact that most prominent voice teachers are women. Ultimately, these forewords highlight what the texts themselves will tell us – that working on the voice is about working on ourselves to become better people.

The reason that we need actually to *work* on our voices is that the modern world has blocked our natural and truthful ones. As Brook's foreword to *Voice and the Actor* summarizes, "Cicely Berry has based her work on the conviction that while all is present in nature our natural instincts have been crippled from birth by many processes – by the conditioning, in fact, of a warped society" (Berry 1973: 3). This fall from Eden is a theme played out through all these texts, but is particularly present in the three later ones. Berry connects our difficulty concerning the speaking of heightened text with the fact that "We live at a time when people are less articulate about their feelings" and that, as we become more educated, "our response to words becomes only literal: we stop feeling the emotional life of the language" (1992: 48). She is even more vehement about this situation in her conclusion to the 1992 reprint of *The Actor and the Text*, focusing particularly on our "product-oriented society" in which television and advertisements have made language "either passive and literal, or to do with selling a commodity" (Berry 1992: 286). Rodenburg also faults the "civilising barriers" of modern life (largely in the form of technological advances like television and a generally chaotic urban culture) that have impeded "language's ancient mesmerising power" (1993: 4–5).

However, although Berry and Rodenburg write of finding your own natural voice, which is free and organic and rid of the problems that block its innate power, the voice they strive to produce is not as neutral as they suggest. Both coaches insist that a good voice is one that is "natural," free of the bad habits and societal forces that have warped our untrained voices: Berry argues that "the condition of life conditions the speech," listing environment, ear, physical agility and personality as the important factors (1973: 7–8); Rodenburg devotes the first part of her book on voice to the myriad "bad habits" that keep us from our "right to speak" (1992: 1–109). For both, the operating paradox is that it is the untrained voice that is constructed, while training recovers the voice's natural state. But the examples Rodenburg invokes of those who have managed to escape "civilising barriers" and have retained access to their powerful, natural voice highlight the ways in which that voice is far from neutral. Rodenburg's continued references to finding vocal power "throughout Africa, India, Aboriginal Australia and the Far East, in small pockets of Europe and in North America among Native American cultures" (Rodenburg 1993: 8), along with her praise of a "Black American gospel singer" (1992: 10–11) and Antony Sher's approving description of Rodenburg as a "pioneer, or missionary, braving real and urban jungles" (Rodenburg 1993: xiv), suggest that what is at stake in a natural voice is a fetishized notion of primitivism, which requires repressed Anglo-American speakers to go in search of a less-cultured expression of emotions. Although it is Rodenburg in particular who is susceptible to this nostalgia for the primitive, Berry also relies on a move towards it: we should stay "free to our basic primitive response" to language, she argues, "primitive in the sense of being less consciously organized, and less culturally based" (1992: 19).

Given this drive, one could imagine that the connection between Shakespeare and voice work is merely coincidental: both Berry and Rodenburg happened to work at a company whose primary focus was Shakespeare. But even that in itself is not coincidental – the RSC had both the resources to hire a full-time voice coach in 1970 and the impetus to create itself as a unified, ensemble company – this reasoning overlooks the degree to which Shakespeare is a central means by which voice work produces healthy, neutral voices. As Knowles points out, British voice coaches long relied on providing actors with voices they could use in a variety of roles and media, and the RSC was striving to present itself as a company whose work could be appreciated by the entirety of Britain, not just the elite (1996: 92–93). Both these factors affected the development of voice work and the belief that Shakespeare's plays represented both the best texts and the most universal characters for the purpose. In fact, given these voice coaches' concerns with a quantifiable quality of text and voice, and their pre-occupation with a common essence that we all have within ourselves, it is hard to imagine their work without Shakespeare.

The combination of the link between voice and self and the import-ance of Shakespeare creates a very specific way of reading the plays. Just as our primitivized self is made "natural" through voice work, so is Shakespeare. Voice work, particularly in its late 1980s and 1990s incarnation, is about making Shakespeare's language "organic," a word that recurs not only in this method but throughout theatre prac-tice. "Organic" is generally used to refer to the way in which everything in a production gives birth to everything else; a good production is then one that forms a coherent and, as the biological metaphor implies, a natural whole. In these books, "organic" refers to the way in which words and voice are physically part of our bodies: Rodenburg insists that "words that respond to need flow through us, practically becoming part of our circulatory system, touching every part of us" (1993: 3) and Berry continually reminds us of the physical response that we can have to words (1992: 19–20). Shakespeare's language too is organic, grounded in the physical reactions of our bodies. "There is no way you can possibly begin to enjoy Shakespeare without speaking him aloud" (Rodenburg 1993: 32), because our physical response to the feeling of speaking his words creates not just our enjoyment, but our understand-ing: "If you speak and sound enough of Shakespeare's texts you will soon understand them with greater ease" (Rodenburg 1993: 170) and "with Shakespeare, more than any other writer, you have to speak the text out loud and feel the movement of the language before you can begin to realize its meaning" (Berry 1992: 52).

The reason that speaking Shakespeare helps us to understand his plays is that the meter and thought patterns of his verse create a bio-logical link between his characters and ourselves. Meter, which is the "cornerstone" of speaking and understanding Shakespeare (Berry 1992: 52), is "organic to the thought" (Berry 1992: 53) and so, gives clues about the character speaking: "when the rhythm breaks within the text it does so because the character, to a large or small degree, is at odds with his [sic] natural rhythm" (Berry 1992: 53). This is not an intellectual reaction to the text, but is linked specifically to the behavior of our bodies. Iambic pentameter, Rodenburg tells us, is "like a heart-beat or the beat of the pulse: the first rhythm we hear in the womb, the last we feel before death" (1993: 136). This is not an unusual way to describe the nature and popularity of iambic pentameter, but for these voice coaches, it is specifically the physical aspect of the meter that makes it a valuable resource for the actor: "Like our inner biology the iambic responds to pressure, tension and stimuli" (Rodenburg 1993: 137). Both we and Shakespeare's characters have pulses that respond to and indicate our emotional states, and it is this pulse that enables an actor to become a character. Even aside from the strict counting of iambs, there are physical connections between the actor and the text through patterns of breathing: "You begin to breathe at the same points as the writer, your heart beats with his or her rhythm, you imaginatively move with the writer across time and space" (Rodenburg 1993: 96).

If this sounds a bit specious, Berry's explanation of the importance of breath patterns is more rooted in language and character analysis. Taking as her starting-point the assertion that breath is "the physical life of the thought" (Berry 1992: 26), she argues that there is an "integration of breath and thought" and that "how we breathe is how we think; or rather, in acting terms, how the character breathes is how the character thinks" (Berry 1992: 26). If we can focus on this integration, we will learn how to think like the character: "we have made the thought our own physically through the breath" and "actually think differently because we are open to the thought in this way" (Berry 1992: 26). Through this method of reading, voice work strives to naturalize Shakespeare, to root the understanding of his language in the physical responses of our bodies.

By making Shakespeare himself part of our natural voice and body, voice teachers seek to empower the actor to wrestle with the plays' language. Both Berry and Rodenburg repeatedly assert that there is nothing to be afraid of in speaking Shakespeare. The language might appear difficult, but it is something that we can all understand since our bodies respond to Shakespeare's words. This desire to make the actor feel comfortable approaching Shakespeare plays a crucial role in how the practice of voice work has developed. Making Shakespeare a part of our bodies has practical and ideological implications for how the plays can be read. A naturalized Shakespeare is not a Shakespeare we are tempted to question. If it's natural, it's good – can we imagine striving for an unnatural Shakespeare? In many ways, the later phase of voice work participates in the American self-help culture of the late 1980s and early 1990s that urged us to get in touch with our emotions and sought to make our emotional and physical lives a coherent whole.[4] Where the catch-phrase of this self-help world was "release your inner child," in voice work it is your inner Shakespeare that you are urged to find.

In effect, Berry and Rodenburg want to heal our twentieth-century neuroses by bringing us closer to the Shakespeare within. Through this physical connection with him, we will learn how to uncover our more primitive voices and selves, uncontaminated by cultural conditioning. This desire for a healthier and more primitive self appears innocent, but it carries an ideological bias that limits the work an actor can do. In voice work, what you discover as your free, individual voice links you both to the common humanity shared by everyone who can strip away their culturally and consciously imposed barriers and to Shakespeare, who is simultaneously you at your individual best and humanity at its collective best. As Knowles argues about these texts, "what 'freedom' will do for actors is to restore a 'natural,' 'childlike' access to 'self,' a psychological 'depth' that puts them in touch with something that is at once their true (individual) selves, our common (universal) humanity, and Shakespeare" (Knowles 1996: 97). This conflation of individual/ universal/Shakespeare naturalizes the social order found in the plays and thwarts challenges to their political tenets. We are Shakespeare; Shakespeare is us. Not only are we not encouraged to be skeptical of the natural, organic Shakespeare that we discover through voice work, the reliance on interpreting individual character's psyches frustrates the ability of the actor to interrogate the larger social structures that shape the depictions of those characters. Instead of the plays deriving from or responding to historically and culturally specific ideologies, they become timeless reflections of our essential human nature. Interpretations grounded in an historicist or materialist framework have no point of entry into voice work's emphasis on the individual self.[5]

That the process of finding our healthy voices leads inexorably to Shakespeare is presented as something that hardly needs comment: "Where voice and text are concerned there is simply no better writer than Shakespeare" (Rodenburg 1993: 167). For Rodenburg, what might sound like a technical assessment of his language skills is revealed to be a judgment of his encompassing humanity:

> It is generally agreed that Shakespeare's plays and sonnets explore with enormous compassion and variety all the great dilemmas facing human beings in conflict. Nothing about the human psyche and human action seemed to escape either his interest or his understanding. When we speak Shakespeare's words today they sound as fresh and meaningful as the day they were written.
>
> (Rodenburg 1993: 167)

The reason that "we *need* Shakespeare" certainly has to do with the fact that he "was a magnificent wordsmith who always perfectly mated the needs of the voice with those of the text" (Rodenburg 1993: 167; emphasis in original), but it is primarily due to his wise insight into human nature. This emphasis on Shakespeare's humanity leads Rodenburg to encourage the actor to "be true to the text and serve its marvels in a variety of circumstances" (Rodenburg 1993: 169). The servitude is not a simple one, however. Throughout her account of the actor's relationship to the text, Rodenburg insists both that actors must be true to the text and that they must bring their own experiences to bear on it. There is a remarkable ambivalence about who is giving voice to whom. On the one hand, "every speaker becomes the new 'author' of a text" (1993: 154); on the other, "The speaker becomes the writer's vessel just as the writer is a vessel of other unseen creative forces" (1993: 96). While an actor's "own *individual* experience of life will cast a unique light on any great text" (1993: 175; emphasis in original), the actor must always be careful that this experience is "used to enhance, not mask, a text's inherent values" (1993: 187). The difference between casting light and masking is not clear, nor is the similarity between the speaker as author and the speaker as vessel. Given the slippage between these areas, and the fact that Rodenburg believes in Shakespeare's wise humanity, it appears that the Bard gives birth to us in the process of our speaking his words. Shakespeare has been waiting for us all this time, understanding and welcoming us no matter who we are:

> Shakespeare's brilliance is that he seems to be able to speak to us all over those hundreds of years and across every cultural bias and barrier. He is a genius because he understands our likenesses as well as our individuality. He touches all who take the time to breathe, speak and need him.
>
> (Rodenburg 1993: 171)

Striking this balance between an actor's individual experience and Shakespeare's inherent values is slightly less tricky in Berry. Berry does not speak, as Rodenburg does, of Shakespeare's greatness; her emphasis is primarily on his language, which "demands such a complete investment of ourselves in the words" (Berry 1992: 9). Perhaps because she has invested less in Shakespeare's great humanity, Berry is more open to actors making their own choices about what the clues in the text tell them and how their roles can be performed. In this open-ended world of possibilities, actors must strive for "a continual blending of our own truth with the truth of the character" (Berry 1992: 15) and "be continually balancing our need to be truthful with a way of presenting that truth to an audience" (Berry 1992: 31). This way of being truthful is less constrained than the need to serve the text by being the author's vessel, but even here there is a contradiction that is not easily reconciled. The point of learning about meter, rhythm and verse structure is that language is where the character resides. The actor "must touch the character through the language" (Berry 1992: 15) for their thoughts "are discovered at the moment of speaking" (105) and "they live where they find their images" (114). Although Berry insists that personal experience and individual choice shape the final decisions of how textual cues are to be performed, she also suggests that there is a natural evolution to the discovery and portrayal of a character. The exercises she has set out for uncovering the various cues in the text will "take on their real significance when you are working in depth on a character, when, hopefully, they will endorse your thinking and your instincts. . . . if you are tuned to all that is happening in the language it will reinforce all you want to do with the character" (Berry 1992: 138). Shakespeare's language will support the actor's characterization, but the "hopefully" in her account of the process suggests that there is a possibility that actors might find themselves at odds with the text.

While both Berry and Rodenburg want to believe in the possibility and ease of combining an actor's individual experience and truth with that of the text, closer examination of this process reveals that it relies on a limiting notion of what Shakespeare can mean. The difficulty of the goal of blending your truth with Shakespeare's is that most directors and producers recognize only specific values as "Shakespearean." Frances Barber's experience of playing Ophelia at the RSC suggests the degree to which one actor's sense of blending truths can be seen by others as distorting Shakespeare's text. When Barber was cast as Ophelia in Ron Daniels' 1984 *Hamlet*, she prepared by "jotting down anything [she] felt personally drawn to in the character" (Barber 1988: 138). After careful reading and rereading, what she finally found was not the typical passive character of most scholarship and theatre histories, but an Ophelia who is Hamlet's "counterpart and counterpoint": "She's full of humour and wit and intelligence, she's strong, courageous, emotionally open. She shows her independence when she gives Hamlet his 'rememberances' back, she stands up to her father, she . . . [*sic*]" (Barber 1988: 139). Despite her textual preparation, when Barber told Daniels of her discovery, as she recounts, he flatly refused to accept it: "Frankie, you *can't* play her as a feminist, it's not in the text" (1988: 139; emphasis in original). Barber describes her defense of her reading ("I had done my justification research rather thoroughly," she tells us) and Daniels' continued resistance:

> "Why does she go mad then?"
> "Because she's the only person in the play who sees what's going on."
> "And?"
> "And she's full of guilt for not having been able to prevent it."
> "And?"
> "And she's full of remorse for her father's death."
> "And?"
> "And she blames herself for Hamlet's prejudice against women."
> "And?"
> "And she's guilt-ridden, Ron! She's utterly guilt-ridden, like every woman I know; and she's culpable up to a point because she knew Claudius and Polonius were spying on Hamlet but she didn't warn him. And she knows he's physically attracted to her and she sort of encourages it."
> "What?"
> "Well I think she does" (my armoury of qualifications in the text was beginning to run a bit thin).
>
> (Barber 1988: 139–40)

Despite all Barber's research and justifications, Daniels would not budge an inch. Eventually, by the end of the run, Barber felt she had been able to make the character her own, but her description of the process shows some of the obstacles that actors can face in reinterpreting characters. Barber's argument with Daniels had little to do with how good a reader she is, but everything to do with how Shakespeare is allowed to be played. Received notions of Shakespeare's female characters can obscure feminist reinterpretations, with unquestioned assumptions about women's behavior replacing textual inquiry and standing in for assertions of universality.

Barber's account suggests how the contest for a universal Shakespeare is consistently configured so that universal equals patriarchal. There are, however, less obvious forces preventing actors from accessing "the universal truth" about their female characters. If actors feel that they must blend their truth with Shakespeare's and achieve a "sense of inner understanding" (Berry 1992: 141), they will try to explain characters' actions and emotions in terms with which they are familiar; the belief that breathing like the characters will enable actors to think and feel like the characters encourages this instinct to understand them through modern analogies. But striving to fit the characters into twentieth-century emotional and psychological paradigms overlooks the vast distance between our own culture and that of the Renaissance, a distance that might alter the fundamental way we think of character and subjectivity. As Catherine Belsey has convincingly argued in *The Subject of Tragedy*, women's confused and fluctuating legal status in the sixteenth and seventeenth centuries resulted in their unstable subject positions. Women's rights fluctuated in part according to their marriage status. Their entitlement to hold property changed depending on whether they had a husband; their accountability when charged with a crime, however, was constant. Even within marriage, a woman's status was not stable. As a wife, a woman had a different role with different rights than as a mother, for example. While a mother was aligned with her husband in ruling as parents over their children, as a wife that same woman was aligned with her children in being subject to their father/husband. Given these contradictions, Belsey finds that women's "relationship to the law in its entirety was paradoxical at best, and unfixed in that it was dependent on their relationship to men" (Belsey 1985: 153). While "the subject of liberal humanism claims to be the unified, autonomous author of his or her own choices (moral, electoral and consumer), and the source and origin of speech" (Belsey 1985: 149), Renaissance women did not have a stable subject-position from which to speak, and "both were and were not subjects" (Belsey 1985: 150). This unstable subjectivity had important consequences for Renaissance drama, in which female characters "speak with equal conviction from incompatible subject-positions, displaying a discontinuity of being, an 'inconstancy' which is seen as characteristically feminine" (Belsey 1985: 149).

Belsey is proposing a two-pronged argument here: that women experienced their own subjectivity in ways different from women today (she claims that a female subject-position comparable to a stable male one did not begin to emerge until the late seventeenth century (1985: 192–221)) and that, because of women's unstable subject-position in the Renaissance, texts of the time represent their utterances as discontinuous. Both sides of this argument complicate the relationship a modern actor has to the female character she is assigned to play. Belsey asserts that our experience of ourselves is fundamentally different from what was available to early modern women, and that our very notions of selfhood and interiority are inapplicable to the Renaissance; an actor cannot simply reproduce the feelings and ways of thinking of a

Renaissance woman, even when breathing like her, because theirs was a radically different (and possibly alienating) experience. Furthermore an actor cannot rely on a character's language to provide insight into those feelings because that language itself participates in the discontinuity of subjectivity. If real Renaissance women had lives that did not correspond to our modern notions of subjectivity, dramatic representations of women are even less likely to be similar. In other words, an actor cannot reproduce in modern terms what the textual clues point to, even if she could decipher them.[6]

These different subject paradigms do not in themselves necessarily pose a problem for acting Shakespeare. Scholars use twentieth-century paradigms to read early modern texts all the time; it would be impossible for a reader not to read texts through his or her contemporary thought system. Critics in the 1990s used feminist theory and practice to investigate the gender relationships in Renaissance drama, though Belsey, for one, argues that feminism itself could not exist before a stable female subjectivity (1985: 150). In this instance, our modern subject-position provides us with a way to analyze and rethink Renaissance relationships. Actors' training, however, does not allow for this sort of investigation. Voice work, like many other modern acting methodologies, does not give actors who are aware of historical differences a way to explore these problems but rather forces them to ignore troubling moments in order to produce an ahistorical connection between actor and character. The resulting narratives tend to emphasize similarities at the expense of discontinuities and to produce characters who appear to be universally accessible. But such character readings, Alan Sinfield argues, are too often predicated on patriarchal assumptions of what is realistic behavior for a woman. Character analyses of Desdemona and Lady Macbeth, he notes, derive from patriarchal stereotypes of normative female behavior:

> Virtually the same pattern is presumed for Lady Macbeth as for Desdemona: initial bold behavior is succeeded eventually by a reversion to "feminine" passivity, with an episode of nagging the husband in between . . . because this sequence seems plausible in our cultures, it seems satisfactory as character analysis, but in fact it is a story about the supposed nature of women. Strength and determination in women, it is believed, can be developed only at a cost, and their eventual failure is at once inevitable, natural, a punishment, and a warning.
>
> (Sinfield 1991: 56)

Character analysis, both the academic kind that Sinfield is considering and the actorly kind that voice work engages in, disassociates dramatic characters from the cultural systems that produce them and, in so doing, elides the operation of forces that feminists would wish to challenge. The answer to Sinfield's riddle, "When is a character not a character?" is "when she or he is needed to shore up a patriarchal representation" (Sinfield 1991: 54).

It is not that actors are unaware of the patriarchal implications of traditional interpretations of Shakespeare's female characters; many actors are explicitly interested in overturning those interpretations and replacing them with their own feminist readings (see, in addition to Barber, Walter 1993 and Rutter 1989). But the process of reading encouraged by voice work trains attention on character motive and emotion, rather than on playwright motive or ideological structure. By reading a play's language as revelatory of a character's feelings and thought processes, voice work ignores the representational and dramaturgical strategies of the text and withholds from actors the tools to deconstruct patriarchal character readings. It focuses on the character at the expense of the play.

The danger of interpreting a character's language as revealing solely his or her emotions becomes clear when we consider Lorraine Helms' understanding of textual clues. Helms notes that today's playscripts bear the traces of textual strategies originally designed to feminize the boy actor, strategies which "may infantilize or eroticize those who now play his roles" (Helms 1994: 108). In other words, where a voice teacher might be inclined to see evidence of a character's thought process in the syntax or rhyme pattern of a soliloquy, Helms would be likely to point to the ways in which the choice of words reflected Shakespeare's need to maintain the female persona of the boy actor. Reading with an awareness of the "politics of prosody," as she terms it, would alter an actor's relationship to the text by providing a new way of interpreting textual clues. Although the clues themselves might stay the same (rhyme, meter, syntactical structures), their organizational framework is different. Helms, for example, reads Cressida's rhyming soliloquies not as evidence of her interior thought processes, but as the textual traces of a system that denied women their own subjectivity and that hinders actors' efforts to access the character's hidden truth:

> Neither the presentational nor representational elements of her speeches encourage her to tell her own history of masculine oppression rather than Troilus's tale of feminine treachery: naturalism may

founder on the artificiality of the rhyme, while a gestic style must overcome the obscurity of the syntax.

(Helms 1994: 121)

Helms' work shows how an analysis of the politics of prosody can help the feminist actor in her Shakespearean work; it also reminds us that considering only character motives obscures the ways in which the playwright's representational project affects textual strategies.

To understand the implications of all this for character reading, I want to return to Alan Sinfield's riddle, "When is a character not a character?" Sinfield's query is part of his contention that character itself is a dramatic strategy that participates in the representation of a patriarchal ideology. Noting that female characters often fall silent at moments that mark "breaking points of the text, moments at which its ideological project is under special strain" (Sinfield 1991: 74), Sinfield concludes that "the presentation of the dramatis personae must be traced to a textual organization in which character is a strategy" that will be abandoned when it interferes with the larger ideological goals of the drama (1991: 78). Edward Burns' history of pre-modern notions of character also describes a dramatic or rhetorical strategy rather than a person with a need for words. While today character is conceived of in a "substantive" mode "as individual and moral essence," the Renaissance was a time when character was "transactional," "a process of knowing" (Burns 1990: 6). Although we have to come to our modern sense of character through Shakespeare and through acting (Burns 1990: 7–8), that sense of substantive character would not have been valid for Shakespeare himself; "for the rhetorical tradition, within which the historical Shakespeare worked, character is a kind of language, and language a kind of action, a social praxis" (Burns 1990: 90). Sinfield and Burns are arguing for an understanding of character as something that *does*, not that *is*: the question to ask is how does a character work, not who a character is.

The emphasis that Belsey, Helms, Sinfield and Burns place on character as an authorial strategy does not mean that characters are only that. A character on stage is produced not only through linguistic effects but through the interaction of those effects with the actor's presence. Characters undoubtedly exist on stage, characters that we read as having an "individual and moral essence." It is folly to imagine a performed Shakespeare that is not received by its audience as concerned with characters. As I will discuss in a later chapter, the presence of actors' bodies onstage signals personhood to modern audiences in ways that literary theorists often do not take into account. But while an audience might infer such notions from actors' performances of Shakespeare's characters, that makes a poor basis for the preparation of a role. An acting method that finds meaning solely within a character's psychology will overlook the ways in which the character's speech (and lack of it) participates in a pattern of meaning that does not reside in plot or character analysis. To insist on the primacy of character is to hide the way that "subjectivity is itself produced, in all of its complexity, within a linguistic and social structure" (Sinfield 1991: 78) and to miss the opportunity to contest the idea of Shakespeare's universal truth.

Where an actor tries to apply voice work in its more practical aspects to a feminist interrogation of Shakespeare, the nature of that work and its commitment to character analysis ultimately limit her effectiveness. By following one actor's course through a role, we can see how and where its parameters operate to determine her performance. Juliet Stevenson is a Royal Shakespeare Company actor who firmly endorses Berry's method: "I believe in what I've been taught by Cis Berry, the RSC's voice teacher – that Shakespeare's characters live in the moment they speak" (Rutter 1989: 43). More than most modern actors, Stevenson seems willing to disregard modern notions of unified character in order to discover what Shakespeare's language indicates, insisting that "the language tells you who the character is moment by moment, word by word. You need not, *should* not, be bound by notions of psychological consistency" (Rutter 1989: 43). But even moving away from a belief in unified character does not open up all the possibilities for a feminist interpretation of a role. Stevenson played Isabella in Adrian Noble's 1983 RSC production of *Measure for Measure*. In Carol Rutter's *Clamorous Voices*, she takes us through her approach to the scene where Isabella has her first interview with Angelo (2.2). Her reading of the exchange bears obvious traces of Berry's influence. She notes that although in her first scene (1.4), Isabella "isn't particularly articulate," she is "released into language by the confrontation with Angelo" (Rutter 1989: 43). When Isabella asks Angelo to spare Claudio's life, the rhythm of the speech tells Stevenson a great deal about her: "I have a brother is condemned to die. / I do beseech you, let it be his fault, / And not my brother" (2.2.34–6). Stevenson's reading of these three lines gives an indication of her mode of examination:

> What she's doing is separating the fault from the man who commits that fault and asking that the fault die and the man live. It's a

philosophical quibble – and she knows it, and the way she says it exposes all her diffidence. It's as though she's trying to rush the sentence past the judge before he spots its legal flaw – getting in there quick with a load of monosyllables and a weak ending, "brother", which trails off, as the line does, into silence. I think Isabella knows her argument is weak. She split her advocacy in two in her opening statement, so there's no strength here, there's no counterbalance. "Die" and "fault" get all the emphasis, metrically and by their position at the end of the line; "brother" has no strength at all. He's not strongly placed in the line, poor bloke.

(Rutter 1989: 45)

This is a fairly straightforward reading of three straightforward lines, but Stevenson's examination of the scene becomes more problematic as it progresses. As the rhythm of the language gets faster, and there are fewer gaps in the meter, Stevenson sees the scene as becoming increasingly sexual:

Their language is so erotic. They keep landing in the middle of each other's thought. He gives her something, and she lands on it, he lands on that, and she lands on *that*. It's such an interdependent development. They're listening so hard to each other. That's partly what's erotic about it: they're receiving each other. And each of them seems, perhaps unconsciously, to be arousing and inflaming the other – propelling each other into ever wider and deeper waters.

(Rutter 1989: 48–9)

Stevenson finally concludes, "She and Angelo have been copulating across the verse ever since they first met" (Rutter 1989: 49). Looking at the language for clues to Isabella's character, Stevenson builds a reading that attributes a fair amount of power to her. Although Isabella might have been unsure of herself in the beginning, here she and Angelo are "interdependent" and "receiving each other." By the end of the scene, Isabella is "on the attack": "She's talking power and she's playing power . . . she's on home ground now" (Rutter 1989: 49).

Stevenson's powerful Isabella was well received by reviewers. In her stage history of Shakespeare's comic heroines, Penny Gay praises this performance as a feminist portrayal:

Stevenson's Isabella was the embodiment of late twentieth-century feminism come of age and accepted into mainstream thinking; her performance enabled audiences to see that a woman's claim for control of her own body is reasonable and normal, and that such autonomy can be a positive force in society.

(Gay 1994: 139)

Gay bases her assessment of Stevenson's performance on her own observations of the production as well as on comments by reviewers such as Andrew Rissik, who writes in *Drama* magazine,

The achievement of the performance is that it turns Isabella into a major dramatic protagonist like Antigone, a woman who says "no" not because of fear or inhibition or downright frigidity but because, in a world whose standards are demonstrably corrupt, she believes "no" to be a test of moral courage and the only right answer.

(Gay 1994: 138–9)

As these responses indicate, a powerful Isabella can be an attractive one for a feminist actor. Certainly an Isabella on the attack makes for a more interesting character to play as well as to watch. A passive Isabella, who is a victim of Angelo's advances, could easily become a one-note performance in this scene, reacting with whatever mixture of horror, fear or resignation the actor feels appropriate. This passive Isabella would also have less performative power – an audience would tend to be more focused on Angelo's actions (with either horror or empathy) than on Isabella's retreat.[7] But an Isabella who talks power and plays power will do as much acting as reacting, and will grab the audience's attention.

Despite the reactions of Gay and others, however, this power-playing Isabella can equally suggest a woman complicit with Angelo's proposition. Reading Isabella's plea to Angelo as "copulating across the verse" sets up a metaphorical copulation that makes the invitation to its physical counterpart seem like a natural, or at least understandable, development. Seeing Isabella and Angelo as "interdependent" suggests that they are equals, and that Angelo's request for sex in exchange for her brother's life could be a reasonable proposition, a transaction between peers. This sexualizing of Isabella could also make the scene easier for viewers. The reactions of some reviewers indicate that their enjoyment of Stevenson's portrayal also involves relief that Isabella was a sexual character. As Gay notes, "relieved that they no longer had to deal with a woman who found the thought of sex revolting, they welcomed the transformation of the role into [quoting reviewer Robert Cushman] 'romantic heroine . . .'" (1994: 138). Gay does not comment that the relieved reviewers were male, but were we to take that into

account, it would appear that they liked Stevenson's Isabella not
because she was an embodiment of modern feminism, but because
they could fall in love with her. Their reaction highlights the
unintended consequences of Stevenson's reading. I do not think that
Stevenson is suggesting that Isabella has asked for Angelo's clearly
unwelcome sexual attention, and she does not claim that the Isabella
who righteously (and rightfully) refuses Angelo's proposal is either at
odds or consistent with the Isabella who was earlier copulating across
the verse with him. But viewers were not forced to question Isabella's
status as desirable; they were invited to share Angelo's desire for her,
rather than explore the implications of that desire. While Stevenson
does not draw a line connecting the powerful and erotic Isabella with
the Isabella subjected to Angelo's harassment, neither she nor the production questions the way in which his proposition seems, though
despicable, also inevitable.

While Stevenson's decision to play Isabella as powerful and erotic
ostensibly stems from Shakespeare's language – "With Shakespeare,
you begin with the words, and you build from there," she argues (Rutter
1989: xvii) – her choice is also a much more consciously ideological
one. She consistently refuses to portray Shakespeare's female characters as helpless victims, for, as she tells Rutter, "That's of no interest
to women, watching women being victims" (Rutter 1989: xxvii). The
rest of her response points to some of the problems with the Isabella
she creates:

> What's interesting is to watch how women collude with what is done
> to them or how they create it, their part in it. Our active participa-
> tion in it is much more interesting to explore than our blamelessness,
> our victimisation. I want women's roles to be as complex in per-
> formance as men's, to restore them to their flawed and rounded
> complexity.
>
> (Rutter 1989: xxvii)

This sounds like an apt description of her Isabella, an active participant in creating her predicament. Stevenson's desire to make the wom-
en's roles complex is certainly understandable, and by no means
incompatible with a feminist agenda. Parading Shakespeare's female
characters across stage as embodiments of women's helplessness and
victimization hardly helps a feminist desire to empower women. But
neither does the option that Stevenson follows. Which is worse, to be
seen as a victim or as a collaborator? The potential conundrum of
Isabella, and many other of Shakespeare's female roles, stems in part

from actors' training. While voice work has given Stevenson the tools with which to recognize the varying speech patterns in Isabella's scenes, it has also ensured that her interpretation of those speech patterns correspond solely to Isabella's emotions. Voice work's focus on a character's words as "a release of the inner life" (Berry 1992: 18) prioritizes character reading above all other avenues of exploration, including consideration of Shakespeare's dramaturgy. The focus is on character, not characterization.

If Stevenson, as trained by Berry, reads the text for clues about Isabella's character, Kathleen McLuskie's cultural materialist method considers Shakespeare's plays in terms of their dramaturgical strategies, looking for "the narrative, poetic and theatrical strategies which construct the plays' meanings and position the audience to understand their events from a particular point of view" (McLuskie 1985: 92). Looking at the same scene through which we traced Stevenson's steps, McLuskie sees not a power balance and interdependence between Isabella and Angelo, but rather a power imbalance, centered on male authority. Isabella, she argues, is "defined theatrically by the men around her for the men in the audience" (McLuskie 1985: 96). In her first plea to Angelo, "she is physically framed by Angelo, the object of her demand, and Lucio the initiator of her plea" (McLuskie 1985: 96). The asides of Lucio and the provost make us want Isabella to win, but Lucio's bawdy innuendos ("Ay, touch him; there's the vein" (2.2.72)) also sexualize Isabella for the audience. The way the scene proceeds encourages the audience to share in Angelo's desire for Isabella, argues McLuskie:

> The passion of the conflict, the sexualising of the rhetoric, and the engagement of the onstage spectators create a theatrical excitement which is necessary to sustain the narrative: it also produces the kind of audience involvement which makes Angelo's response make sense.
>
> (McLuskie 1985: 96)

Although both McLuskie and Stevenson highlight the erotic energies of the scene between Angelo and Isabella, they differ in their interpretation of that eroticism: the end result, according to McLuskie, is a circumscription of Isabella's agency, and not the movement toward power that Stevenson sees. Rather than locating Isabella's sexuality in her choice of words, McLuskie attributes that erotic energy to character depiction. Using this approach to the scene, an actor might find a way around the question of victim or collaborator, asking instead how best to work with or against those authorial strategies that frame her as erotic.

But it is no simple matter for an actor to adopt this non-character-based manner of reading. An important aspect of the difference between Stevenson's focus on character emotions and McLuskie's on dramaturgical devices is not methodological but ideological: while Stevenson trusts Shakespeare, McLuskie does not. Both Stevenson and McLuskie define themselves as feminists concerned with Shakespeare's female characters. But where Stevenson inevitably comes back to the fact that you must trust Shakespeare's script and that in his words you can uncover strong women that have been hidden by years of theatrical and interpretive tradition (she is interested in "clearing away the rubble of tradition that threatens to bury the roles" and in "reinvestigating Shakespeare's women from scratch" (Rutter 1989: xiii, xviii)), McLuskie is profoundly suspicious of any attempt to recuperate Shakespeare as a feminist. She sees his scripts as inevitably patriarchal, born of a wholly male entertainment industry that reproduces misogynist stereotypes: the plays' textual strategies "limit the range of meaning which the text allows and circumscribe the position which a feminist reader may adopt *vis-à-vis* the treatment of gender relations and sexual politics within the plays" (McLuskie 1985: 92). Stevenson's reading of Shakespeare strives to adapt him for feminist actors, to incorporate her feminist values into his body of work. McLuskie, on the other hand, desires "the power of resistance, subverting rather than co-opting the domination of the patriarchal Bard" (1985: 106).

These significant differences are rooted in the institutional affiliations of McLuskie and Stevenson. As an actor who performs in mainstream theatre tradition, Stevenson is bound by the conventions and beliefs of that tradition, including the convention of naturalistic or truthful acting and a belief in the genius of Shakespeare. As Denis Salter points out, an actor's desire to be natural is entirely reasonable:

> Nobody, except perhaps madmen, children, criminals, and revolutionaries, wants to behave unnaturally – actors least of all. Their skill in animating a role and their popularity with audiences depend, of course, on how successful they are in realizing tacitly understood beliefs about what constitutes a "natural" performance.
>
> (Salter 1996: 116)

By contrast, "Acting Shakespeare *un*naturally is . . . a very dangerous thing to do" (Salter 1996: 117; emphasis in original). For an actor, to be unnatural is to run the risk of losing future employment; for an actor interested in classical theatre, deviating from a natural and universal Shakespeare is to double that risk. If an actor were publicly and consistently to debunk the myth of Shakespeare's value, she or he would soon be cast off the stages of the RSC, which relies precisely on the financial benefits of a belief in Shakespeare's universal value (see chapter 2). The desire to act Shakespeare naturally, then, is sensible and, indeed, natural. Academia, on the other hand, is much more tolerant of work that debunks Shakespeare. Certain current schools of criticism value skepticism over bardolatry. Also, universities' system of employment allows some professors a security that reduces the danger of their skepticism. Tenured professors can espouse potentially risky views (such as discrediting Shakespeare, which would seem to destroy the livelihood of so many academic critics who teach and write on his works) while still expecting a future income; untenured professors, of course, are not necessarily so free.

The differences I have sketched between Stevenson and McLuskie should not be seen as discrediting either of their methodologies or as being limited to them alone. The tension between the views espoused by academia and theatre has had a profound effect on how the two branches of the Shakespeare industry have shaped themselves and makes it difficult for one side to adopt the practices or beliefs of the other. While voice work is imbued with the theatrical values of its originating moment, it is also embedded in the struggle between theatre practitioners and academics for authority over Shakespeare. Christopher McCullough's examination of "the Leavis connection" with the RSC illuminates some of this contest for authority. As he points out, the RSC's first two artistic directors, Peter Hall and Trevor Nunn, both went to Cambridge and studied under F. R. Leavis, and both "have specifically cited Leavis as one of the most important influences on their work as directors of Shakespearean theatre" (McCullough 1988a: 113). There is, however, an inherent contradiction in drawing on Leavis for inspiration for the RSC:

> There is a fundamental irony in Hall looking to Leavis as a mentor in the search for a methodology to reproduce Shakespeare (theatrically) as a "relevant" component of a national culture. The emphasis from Cambridge English and Leavis was that national culture was embodied in the "constant" form of literature. Leavis possessed a strong antipathy to the idea of performance, never more strongly

expressed than when the "performance" entailed the appropriation of a literary text.

(McCullough 1988a: 116)

As Barbara Hodgdon summarizes, Leavis creates a polar relationship between performer and reader, "opposing the self-insistent performer who imposes meanings on a text to the subservient reader who locates meanings in the precise letter of the text," despite the fact that he was himself a performer in his lectures and tutorials (Hodgdon 1994: 260). Hodgdon, like McCullough, describes the "Leavisite reading strategies" that are the foundation of the RSC's rehearsal work as an ironic presence, given Leavis' antitheatricality (Hodgdon 1994: 263). But this anti-theatricality is precisely why the RSC, through voice work, has produced its own version of Leavis' textual scrutiny: by mirroring academic reading strategies, the RSC is able to co-opt and neutralize any accompanying disdain for theatre.

In the 1960s and 1970s particularly (and continuing through to the present), the RSC was concerned to confirm itself as a cultural custodian of Shakespeare, a repository of his moral values that deserved to be supported by the government. By wresting away from academics the claim of authority over Shakespeare's works, the RSC could award itself an institutional status similar to that of Oxford and Cambridge. Just as the great universities were handing on Shakespeare's genius to future generations, so was the RSC; and by virtue of being a popular theatre that all classes could (and would) attend, the RSC had the potential to spread Shakespeare to a larger number of people than universities could. As Alan Sinfield points out in his examination of the "Shakespeare-plus-relevance" ethos that was the driving factor behind the first decades of the company's productions, "The RSC has, from the start, fostered this potent combination of relevance and the real Shakespeare by announcing its respect for the scholarship which seems to authenticate the process" (Sinfield 1985: 175; see also McCullough 1988a: 117). In reproducing the acknowledged methods of academia through voice work, the RSC could claim the authority of the university for itself. And by successfully using academic methods that argue against the validity of theatrical performance, the RSC could demonstrate the fallacy of Leavis' antitheatrical discourse.

The most important aspect of voice work in this regard is not that it reproduces academic methods, but that it claims that the goals of those methods are in fact best realized by actors. Voice work takes the essentially literary process of close reading and brings it into a theatrical context, justifying its move by accepting the premise that Shakespeare's meaning resides in the close examination of his text and then arguing that actors have a closer affinity to the text than academics. Berry's *The Actor and the Text* is a clear example of this recontextualization. Berry's attention to Shakespeare's text covers in detail a range of literary tropes: she names and scans a variety of metrical forms, discusses feminine endings, rhymes, the use of antithesis. Her textual scrutiny clearly mirrors that of academic practitioners. At the same time, however, she insistently reminds us that we must not have an "over-educated response" to Shakespeare's language (Berry 1992: 22–3), ensuring that her reproduction of academic methodology cannot be understood as an endorsement of scholars' right to access Shakespeare over the right of theatre practitioners. As she concludes, "we in the theatre retain the power to excite people with language; it should not be owned by the educated and/or those who rule" (Berry 1992: 285). While agreeing with the aims of academic methodology, she insists that actors are best able to realize those aims. The true discovery of Shakespeare's meaning, as we have seen, lies in our physical response to the words – you have to feel his language "knocking around inside you" before you can sense his meaning (Berry 1992: 52) – and without this physical response you are likely to impose your own sense rather than listen to Shakespeare's. In order truly to understand words, we have to "make them part of our whole physical self in order to release them from the tyranny of the mind" (Berry 1992: 22; Rodenburg also speaks specifically of "The Tyranny of the Intellectual" (1993: 44–5)). This is the move that reformulates Leavis' opposition of self-insistent performer and subservient reader. Like Leavis, Berry agrees that we must be true to the letter of Shakespeare's text rather than selfishly impose our own readings on top of it, but Berry inverts Leavis' hierarchy; it is only the performer who can ultimately be true to Shakespeare's language, while the intellectual reader will forever be distanced from Shakespeare's real meaning.[8]

Voice work's adoption of academic reading habits, however, does not erase academic claims to Shakespeare; for all its protestations that the plays are better realized on stage than in the reader's study, textual scrutiny insistently brings theatre practitioners back to the primacy of the book. As Douglas Lanier recognizes, "recasting the text as a theatrical 'score' paradoxically invests the text with even more authority, with the consequence that its every jot and tittle articulate a theatrical intent that any given enactment can only aspire to" (Lanier 1996: 190).[9]

But while performed Shakespeare is always drawn back to the experience of reading, academic Shakespeare is increasingly being drawn back to the text's performative origins. The rise of performance criticism, argues Lanier, coincides with a move away from the cultural supremacy of the book, now under threat in this age of film and video: "once Shakespeare is (re)grafted on to performative media or textual documents (re)conceived as performative scores or unique artifacts, he and the cultural capital he represents can be uncoupled from the decline of the book in an increasingly post-literate society" (Lanier 1996: 191). If voice work fetishizes the text and the discovery of Shakespeare within its clues, academics are susceptible to fetishizing performance and the possibilities inherent in it: discovering Shakespeare's "real" meaning, enabling social revolution, revitalizing literacy. Many current performance scholars retain their skepticism, just as some voice coaches retain theirs in the face of voice work's essentialist claims, but the circular exchange of authority that Lanier presents suggests that both sides long for what each imagines the other has.[10]

This contest over access to Shakespeare's meaning affects the practice of acting and the related struggle between actor and playwright for control over the performance (see Worthen 1997: 95–150). Voice work insists that actors remain true to Shakespeare and his text: they respond to his clues, allow his language to enter their bodies. But while the premise of voice work assumes a set of textual clues that determine a character's nature, it also allows that there is no single correct performance of a character. The reason that every individual performance will be different and that every new characterization will be fresh is that although you must be true to Shakespeare, you must be true to yourself as well. There is some anxiety around this issue in Berry's and Rodenburg's texts, which insist paradoxically that the more you obey Shakespeare's clues, the more freedom you have. As Rodenburg urges, "Trust the need and fully speak his words and you will stay in control. Not your version of control but his" (Rodenburg 1993: 172). To find yourself, you must submit to Shakespeare; to be in control, you must be in his control.

Actors need Shakespeare, of course, to legitimize their performances. Actors are expected to bring this author – more than any other playwright – to life: Shakespeare is true, Shakespeare is wise, Shakespeare is a 400-year-old cultural icon that transient mortal actors must serve the best they can. Authorizing their performance choices as Shakespeare's is the best defense actors have against spectators' criticisms. Relying on Shakespeare's clues is also the best defense voice coaches have as they tread the sometimes dangerous territory between director and actor. When Cicely Berry became the first voice coach to have a full-time affiliation with the RSC (and indeed, the first full-time voice coach affiliated with any British theatre company (Parker 1985: 32)), she found that she had to create a niche for herself that would not disturb the directors there: "Directors were very suspicious. It took me seven or eight years before nobody questioned what I was going to do with [the actors]" (Parker 1985: 32).

Gradually Berry did, of course, come to be accepted and valued within the RSC, but the path of the voice coach can still be an uneasy one. In our 1995 interview, Jane Boston, a voice teacher at the Central School for Speech and Drama, described the relationship between director and voice coach as "contentious" and "explosive" (Boston 1995); she laughed when saying this, but was also very serious. She attributes the tensions in the relationship partly to gender dynamics and also, historically, to the fact that voice coaches still bear the evolutionary traces of their origins in the elocution teacher. The most prominent voice coaches today are women, while most directors of Shakespeare are still men.[11] This does not pass unnoticed: in his foreword to *The Right to Speak*, Ian McKellen comments that in his professional career he has been "crucially helped" by four voice teachers, all of whom were women. The reason for this remained a mystery to him, he says, until he read Rodenburg's book and realized that "its title is born of a feminist determination to realise a person's individuality" (Rodenburg 1992: viii). But the gendering of voice work is likelier to be the result of the history of elocution teachers; Berry worked in a private studio before being appointed to the RSC and both she and Rodenburg still give private lessons in addition to their work at theatre companies and drama schools. Voice coaches have been figured as enablers (they help the actors to do their jobs) rather than as determiners (the province of the director), a configuration that both reflects and contributes to the gendering of the work. The female voice coach might be invited into the rehearsal room at the male director's behest, that is, allowed into his territory as long as he feels her work is valuable. Actors might also seek out a voice coach individually for private sessions, an arrangement reminiscent of the lessons elocution teachers would hold in their homes.

The status of voice work as an interloper in the rehearsal process is reflected in the characterization of it as a neutral tool that helps the actor discover Shakespeare's clues rather than as an interpretive process that helps the actor discover his or her own reading of the text. Just as the claim that they are responding to clues embedded in the script allows actors to ward off accusations that their interpretations are invalid, so the authority of Shakespeare allows voice coaches to ward off complaints from directors that they are interfering in the creative process of a production. If actors' institutional parameters determine their possible choices in performing Shakespeare, voice coaches' institutional status similarly determines how they teach Shakespeare. The constant reminders that acting Shakespeare is not difficult ("I do not want this attention to detail to make our work seem difficult, because it is not" (Berry 1992: 100)) not only encourage actors to feel empowered but validate the drama-school-trained voice coach in the face of the university-educated director.[12] Particularly at the RSC, which positioned itself explicitly as a Cambridge heir to Shakespeare theatre, such insistence on the ability of actors to understand Shakespeare also justifies the practice of the voice coaches themselves.

As the tension between male academics and female voice specialists has shaped the practice of voice work, so it has diminished its reception outside the studio and rehearsal room. Evidence of the impact of voice work's gendering is seen in its representation in studies of the rehearsal methods of the RSC, which focus on the work done by John Barton to the exclusion of Cicely Berry's influence on the company. Sally Beauman's history of the RSC does not mention Berry once, while Alan Sinfield, Christopher McCullough and Barbara Hodgdon all cite Barton as evidence of the company's close-reading methods (Sinfield 1985: 175, McCullough 1988a: 117, Hodgdon 1994: 264). These last three critics are specifically interested in the way in which the RSC has appropriated academic methodologies for its rehearsal work, and presumably focus on Barton, a former Cambridge don, because he more readily proves their point about the Cambridge connection. But the absence of Berry from their citations of the RSC's rehearsal process indicates the general lack of awareness outside the theatre industry of voice work's contribution to current acting methodology. It is only very recently that Berry has become a focus of attention for academics, a move that reflects a shift towards a larger awareness of performance criticism and the entrance of theatre practitioners into the world of Shakespeare scholarship. Much of the current focus on Berry and other voice coaches can be traced directly to an article by Richard Paul Knowles (published in 1996 but circulated in manuscript since 1993). Knowles is interested specifically in the practice of voice training, but he is uniquely aware of the gender implications of voice work, arguing that Berry's influence on the company "has been significantly more direct than that of Brook, or arguably of any other single figure, though as a voice coach (gendered female) she has been less celebrated" (Knowles 1996: 95).[13]

The single figure who has most often eclipsed Berry in academic notice remains John Barton, whose immensely popular *Playing Shakespeare* both reflects and contributes to this imbalance. Filmed as a series of workshops for Britain's Channel 4 Television in 1984, its origins were a two-part series on "the difficulties and techniques of speaking verse" made for London Weekend Television in 1980 (Barton 1984: viii). This earlier series was made up of workshops led by Trevor Nunn (then Artistic Director of the RSC), Barton, Terry Hands and a group of RSC actors. Despite the fact that Berry had been part of the company since Nunn hired her in 1970, she was not apparently a participant. In Nunn's foreword to the published edition of *Playing Shakespeare*, he credits the series with revealing "the method and principle of an approach to acting Shakespeare which has been fundamental to the Royal Shakespeare Company since it was formed" (Barton 1984: viii). Many of the methods explicated in the series have the same philosophy and practice as those put forward by Berry.

I am not claiming that either Berry or Barton invented the practice of voice work. But, until Knowles, the practice had come to be associated solely with Barton in a move that replicates the contest for authority over Shakespeare staged in Berry's voice work. As a male director who studied and taught at Cambridge, Barton claims more authority over Shakespeare's meaning than Berry is able to as a woman trained at the Central School for Speech and Drama. Barton himself adds to his mantle of authority by specifically linking his work as a director with Shakespeare's own work. Throughout *Playing Shakespeare* he describes the playwright as directing the actor through clues in the text: "Shakespeare *is* his text. So if you want to do him justice, you have to look for and follow the clues he offers. If an actor does that then he'll find that Shakespeare himself starts to direct him" (Barton 1984: 168; emphasis in original). If Shakespeare is a director, then Barton is a present-day Shakespeare, a modern reincarnation of the bard (Nunn actually describes Barton as "the young man with the Renaissance face" (Barton 1984: vii)). In contrast, neither Berry nor Rodenburg use the metaphor of Shakespeare directing the actor. Rather than being directed, actors learn to recognize the textual cues that blend with their own inner selves. Berry and Rodenburg link themselves metaphorically with the actor, not Shakespeare, and actors' accounts of working with them suggest that they are seen as extensions of the actor's work, not the director's. The connection of voice work to Barton rather than Berry also replicates the contest between feminist interrogations of the play and a universal Shakespeare. Just as voice work teaches that there is a timelessly true Shakespeare, whose universal appeal encompasses and supercedes any particular cultural structures, Barton's public face as the interpreter of the universal Shakespeare takes precedence over Berry's more local, private coaching of actors. Together, these emphases on the universal suggest that work done by women is supplementary at best – the real work on Shakespeare is done by men. This vision permeates the RSC.

2

Punching Daddy, or the politics of company politics[1]

The RSC Women's Group has its origins in a weekend devoted to women's theatre work during the Fourth RSC / W. H. Smith Festival in the autumn of 1985. The Fortnight, as the festival was called, was a two-week event sponsored by W. H. Smith and created and run by RSC actors. According to Fiona Shaw, a member of the organizing committee, that year "it was agreed that rather than have the thing overburdened with the majority of men which were in the company, that there would be a special weekend held for the women, of which Juliet [Stevenson] and I were put in charge."[2] Shaw and Stevenson had become friends through that season's *As You Like It*, in which they played Celia and Rosalind. During rehearsals, they had focused on the relationship between their characters and the implications of their great friendship giving way to separate marriages.[3] Their investigation into the construction of Shakespeare's female characters grew to include the rest of their work at the RSC, including the Fortnight. Shaw specifically pinpoints their production of *As You Like It* as the start of the Women's Group: "It really came out of myself and Juliet meeting and having such fantastic conversations." Although the leadership of the RSC subsequently questioned the Group's relevance to Shakespeare, the women behind its formation saw the two as fundamentally connected.

During the course of planning for The Fortnight's Women's Weekend, Shaw and Stevenson continued their conversations with other women in the company, holding meetings to discuss the relationship between feminism and theatre. The weekend itself was seen as a chance to focus on women directors in Britain and, in Shaw's words, to invite them all "to come to Stratford and knock on the door." Although not many directors came, the weekend, on 19–20 October 1985, maintained this goal of improving opportunities for women within mainstream theatre. The first day of the Women's Weekend was devoted to plays performed and devised by women in the company, and the second to talks and debates about women's roles in theatre. Julia Pascal, writing in *City Limits*, described this final day as follows:

> Writer and historian Sheila Rowbotham spoke of the recent history of the women's movement and touched on the need for taking space in a culture dominated by men. Helen Carr, one of the three editors of the new magazine *Women's Review*, talked of the role of language, power and gender. But the afternoon was an open forum which took the debate away from academic analysis into a more pragmatic arena. What can actresses do in a power structure where the artistic control is dominated by white Oxbridge men? The debate explored the problems actresses encounter when they are not allowed to be directed by an equal quota of female directors. As Fiona Shaw said, "What is being said at the RSC is that a good director is a male and a bad director is a female. The hiring system tells you that. We want to do something to redress that balance." This provocative day raised questions about inequality which will have to be answered.
>
> (Pascal 1985)[4]

Both Rowbotham's and Carr's talks covered subjects directly related to the work Shaw and Stevenson had been doing in *As You Like It*, but the afternoon session was most closely linked to the emerging Women's Group and its concern with the lack of opportunities for women at the RSC. For the group, the answer to the questions Pascal highlights seems to lie in the direction of Shaw's comment: substitute women for men. But while hiring female directors might have seemed radical to the men in charge of the company, simply substituting female directors for male directors would do nothing to redress the inequality of power within the company's decision-making hierarchy.

Although the RSC appeared to be caught off guard by the Women's Group's complaints, the absence of women in positions of power was a growing concern, not only within the company but throughout the theatre community. In January 1984 the Conference of Women Theatre Directors and Administrators (CWDTA) released *The Status of*

Women in British Theatre, 1982–83, which found that "the more money
and more prestige a theatre has, the less women will be employed as
directors and administrators; the less likelihood that a play written by a
woman will be commissioned or produced, excepting Agatha Christie;
and the less [*sic*] women there will be on the Board" (Parrish 1984: b).
The implications of this are profound, concluded the survey's author:

> These facts taken together confirm that women are the least subsid-
> ised artists and workers in the theatre. This raises serious questions
> about equality of opportunity; of expression. This has in turn fun-
> damental implications for the legitimate aspirations of women in
> theatre: for women directors to direct Shakespeare, and other clas-
> sics, which are also their heritage: for women writers to write plays
> for main stages: for women actors to be offered parts which extend
> beyond playing a man's mother, wife, mistress, sister or daughter:
> and for women administrators to run their departments as equals,
> not as super secretaries, in whichever structures they choose.
>
> (Parrish 1984: c)

In summarizing the CWDTA report for *Drama* magazine, Sue Dunderdale emphasized that since women are part of the public which funds
these theatres, they deserve to have equal access to those funds (Dunderdale 1984: 11); Fiona Shaw echoed this point when she described
the basis of the Women's Group as "a feeling that the RSC, which was
a subsidized company by a country that was 53 per cent women, would
somehow reflect the preoccupations of the country totally."

As the earlier CWDTA report and the RSC's own history indicate,
the complaints from the Women's Group should not have been
unexpected. Although women had been directing in Stratford-upon-
Avon at the Shakespeare Memorial Theatre for some time – four productions of Shakespeare were directed by women between 1939 and
1956 – they had been almost completely absent from Stratford's directorial posts since the formation of the RSC in 1961.[5] At the time the
Women's Group began in 1985, only one woman had made any sort of
impact on the RSC. Buzz Goodbody was an important part of the
company until her death in 1975, directing four Shakespeare and three
non-Shakespearean plays, assisting on six more plays, expanding
Theatregoround (the RSC's educational theatre program) and develop-
ing The Other Place.[6] But subsequent female directors Penny Cherns,
Sheila Hancock, Gillian Lynne and Di Trevis did only one or two
productions each (including those co-directed with a man) and only
Hancock and Trevis had directed Shakespearean plays, both for the

RSC's national tour, Hancock in 1983 and Trevis in 1985.[7] The CWDTA report reveals this predominantly male pattern of employment extending to the RSC's administration, finding that in the 1982–3 season, the artistic, associate and resident directors were all men, three of the four assistant directors were men, the top administration was entirely male, and sixty of the seventy board members were men (Parrish 1984: 12).

The RSC women continued their meetings after The Fortnight's Women's Weekend was over. These eventually culminated in a meeting with Terry Hands, then co-Artistic Director, shortly before the company moved down to London at the end of the year. Fiona Shaw, Susan Todd (who was to join the group as their director) and Genista McIntosh (who had been the RSC Planning Controller from 1978 to 1984 and who rejoined the RSC in 1985 as Senior Administrator) all describe a scenario in which the women, in McIntosh's words, "threw down a gauntlet" (Goodman 1993b: 217) and Hands was made to respond. Hands, however, describes the meeting as something which he initiated and of which he was in control. Saying he had been aware of grumblings about the lack of opportunities for women within the RSC, he called a meeting of all the women in the Stratford company in which he addressed them, "trying to give a historical perspective and equally admitting that there was something that should be done." He suggested that the women do a company project, similar to the RSC's work on *Nicholas Nickleby*, and recommended that they work with the Laxdaela saga, a thirteenth-century text about the founding of Iceland. He also told them he would support whatever they thought worthwhile: "if there are other things you want to do, authors you want to commission, projects you want to set up, I will make sure the RSC financially backs it, provides the spaces, and so on and so forth."

Hands describes himself as a facilitator: the women had complaints, so he wanted to give them a way of solving the problem. McIntosh explains the dynamics between the women and Hands rather differently: "Because he's quite devious and quite clever . . . he kind of nodded in their direction without ever really putting anything tangible behind it." In the end, she says, "it was probably misguided to imagine that they were ever really being given permission to do anything much." In retrospect, it is unclear exactly what Hands was facilitating. He saw the women's demands, essentially, as coming from a desire for better parts; in his eyes, their frustrations were not so much gender-specific, but actor-specific. He realized he had to hire women to direct and manage the project ("Necessarily I said to them you've got to organize it. I'm a man, I can't do that for you."), but he did not see the group as anything other than a chance to create a piece of theatre with strong roles for women.

A few months after the meeting with Hands, Fiona Shaw, Juliet Stevenson and Lindsay Duncan gave an interview in which they criticized the RSC for the paucity of women in positions of power within the company.[8] In an article about the interview, *Stage and Television Today* reporter Angela Thomas claimed that "Their remarks are being widely seen as a symptom of the growing discontent of women about the lack of opportunities for them in the theatre" and summarized the actors' complaints as follows:

> In an interview with *Theatregoer Magazine*, the three actresses have highlighted the need for more women directors within subsidised theatre as well as the lack of any female influence on major policy decisions. They also claim that the RSC's so called "women's project" was purely a reaction to another article which criticized the lack of women in the company. And they noted that the men at the top were more willing to give an inexperienced man, whether writer or director, rather than a woman the chance to learn his craft within the company.
>
> (Thomas 1986)

Hands was reportedly furious with the actors and, says Shaw, sent them each "an incredibly cross memo – for a moment we thought we were all going to lose our jobs." Hands' sensitivity to their public criticisms (according to Shaw he felt that "we had washed our dirty linen in public") stemmed from his feeling that the company was under siege from the press, and that they were facing enough difficulties without the actors adding to it. The 1985/6 and 1986/7 seasons were extremely difficult ones, with theatre attendance at the Barbican Theatre at half their usual levels (Royal Shakespeare Company 1987a). In addition to struggling to stay afloat with this reduced income, the RSC faced problems with the *Sunday Times'* accusations of financial mismanagement against their recently departed co-Artistic Director, Trevor Nunn. Hands felt that the controversy over Nunn was part of a calculated attack by Rupert Murdoch's newspapers (which include the *Sunday Times*) on the RSC and on theatre as a whole; he felt as well that the Conservative government, which was drastically cutting theatre funding across the board, supported Murdoch's accusations. Although Hands says he has no specific recollection of the *Theatregoer* interview or his reaction to it, he does agree that in light of press hostility and the

RSC's financial crisis, he was likely to have been angry with the three actors:

> When anybody, male or female, chooses that moment to rock the boat, the timing is not appropriate. And it's not appropriate when you've actually said to them, "look have your own group, do your own thing" and they don't do it. That's when confused thinking becomes dangerously naive. And as you would with a child, you smack its bottom.

Hands' use of a parental metaphor reveals the degree to which his view of the RSC as a family affected the dynamics of the company's operation. As he told Christopher McCullough in an interview a few years after this incident, "Our organization is built on personal relationships, making the whole structure analogous to a family. As a family we have our problems and our tensions, but we work together with the common aim of providing a service to the public" (McCullough 1988b: 124). Susan Todd suggests that the uproar over the interview was related to this family dynamic: "They hate it at the RSC when any members of the company speak out. It works on loyalty very much; very familial." This patriarchal structure of the RSC, in which the father is always in charge, played an important role in determining what opportunities women had and how they reacted to the company. Colin Chambers, writing in 1980, describes a family culture that could at times be stifling:

> The metaphor that still occurs is that of the family, and the traditional implications hold true. The Company remains a male-dominated hierarchy, with those who are definitely parents and those who are definitely children (and if they happen to be secretaries and women, which is most often the case, they will be servicing their wise, humanist "fathers" with cups of tea or coffee). The family asks for and expects loyalty, but looks after those it considers its own, especially in dealing with "outsiders" like the Arts Council. It is riven by rows, and a lot depends on personality, though in public the family keeps face.

> (Chambers 1980: 17)

Chambers' perception of the paternalism of the RSC makes highly plausible the idea of the women in the company wanting to rebel while also indicating how notions of loyalty could complicate revolutionary desires. Hands' own description of RSC family values paints a much more positive picture of how cozy the company could be:

It was in those days very very much a collaborative organization, and people really were sounding boards for each other, and critics for each other, and helpers in terms of crisis and need. So it was a good place to work on many levels. It was very very much a family. And you would have disputes, catastrophes, and wonderful moments of joint celebration.

It was also, according to Hands, a family in a more literal sense, "a place where a lot of people had babies" and where there was "a family in the creche and the kind of bubbly life." Hands' vision of a place where actors could go to have babies (because the company offered a contract of two years' steady income) is a pleasant one: the RSC as a place that supports its actors precisely because it is the parent and they are the children.

Chambers' and Hands' contrasting interpretations of the RSC family suggest the ambivalent feelings of women in the organization. In many ways, the relationship between Hands and the Women's Group played itself out along the lines of a *paterfamilias* and his rebellious adolescent children. Everyone I spoke to about the group brought up the idea of the RSC as a family of his or her own accord – it was clearly fundamental to the working methods and vision of the RSC, as well as to the women's desires to rebel (or not to rebel, in some cases) against that structure. McIntosh speaks of the RSC of the 1970s and 1980s as being a patriarchal organization, "in the sense that the company was, and to some extent remains, obsessed by its history and its sense of being a family organization," and Shaw's description of the group's relationship with Hands certainly echoes that family atmosphere: "You see we were always maneuvering, wondering whether we were affecting him here, and actually he may have been oblivious most of the time. There was a sense of punching Daddy." For the members of the group, their status as actors defined them as children and their status as women within the patriarchal structure doubly reinforced their distance from the source of power.

As the furor over the interview died down, the women began following up Hands' invitation to put something together for the winter 1986 Pit season. It was at this point that Susan Todd joined the Women's Group. Todd should have been a good fit with the group. She had a long history with feminist theatre, having been a founding member of the Women's Street Theatre Group, the Women's Company and Monstrous Regiment, and a regular participant in the Women's Theatre Group.[9] She also had a history of connections to the RSC. She was an assistant director to John Barton in 1968/9 and was one of the first women directors inside the Barbican, brought in by McIntosh and the actor Harriet Walter to direct a production of Shirley Gee's *Typhoid Mary* for the Barbican One Year On Festival in March 1983. Out of this production grew a friendship with Juliet Stevenson (who had played Mary) and her later involvement with the Women's Group. When the group started looking for a piece to do, Stevenson came to Todd to discuss the project. Todd does not know whether Stevenson had wanted to invite her to join them or merely to use her as a sounding board, but her initial reaction was

> a very mixed one of irritation, annoyance, rage that this big institu-
> tion, of which I had been part in my early days as a director, was
> wanting to reach out to embrace what it saw as the latest fashionable
> something, the latest idea that they couldn't really ignore any longer.

Todd was determined to be part of it: "I thought, 'Well if there's bloody well going to be resources available to do a feminist piece at the RSC, I'm bloody well going to do it.'" Regardless of whether Stevenson was intending to ask her to join the project or not, Todd made it quite clear that she thought she deserved to be in on it:

> I think I probably laid down the law and was very dogmatic about it.
> I'm sure that I gave Juliet to understand that if any such thing was
> going to happen that I should certainly be involved in it, because I
> considered myself to be, and indeed I was, a leading figure in
> feminist theatre at that point.

Todd's initial impression of the Women's Group when she first met them, around March or April 1986, was that the actors had little in common other than "a kind of vague feminism" and "considerable discontent at the poverty of roles assigned to them within the company in every respect." Although she could sympathize with their feelings of marginalization, she also saw it as the inevitable result of being in the RSC: "you're talking four or five women's roles for every twenty-five men's roles; that is the way it is in a classical company." Todd's impatience with their political sense is tied to her own sense of the proper way to be a female artist:

> I regarded the women within the RSC with a certain amount of
> healthy suspicion, in the sense that they could not but be women
> who were striving to fulfill their ambitions within a very male-
> dominated domain. And they had not, up to that point, struck out

for themselves into the feminist domain, and discovered what it was to work autonomously as a female artist.

If, as some have suggested, Todd was jealous of not having had the chance to become part of the RSC as a young director, she might have felt that her own experience as a struggling (albeit also important) fringe director justified her impatience with what she saw as these women's comfortable, nationally subsidized artistic lives. If she had had to struggle in order to realize her feminist politics, then it might have been tempting to see these women, who were outside the feminist theatre movement, as having only the vaguest kind of political awareness. Todd's frustration with the group's lack of feminist savvy is not necessarily reflective of the group's experience of itself: Shaw remembers those early meetings as "intellectually very vibrant" and "terribly exciting," full of the sense that "we were changing the world."

Regardless of such differences in perception, Todd thought the group's lack of feminist theatre experience was a hindrance to their effectiveness in creating a feminist project. Her emphasis on being an autonomous female artist illustrates how the women at the RSC found themselves politically and artistically without foundation. Not only was the RSC not an institution that encouraged feminist exploration, feminist theatre rarely accommodated traditional drama. Todd's skepticism about female artists working within a male tradition is shared by many within the worlds of feminist theatre and scholarship. In her important history of modern British feminist theatre, Lizbeth Goodman excludes work done by female actors in male-authored scripts, implying that the only valid arena for feminist theatre practitioners is within female-anchored projects, where women are the actors, directors and playwrights (Goodman 1993a: 29). And in one of the foundational texts of feminist theatre scholarship, Sue-Ellen Case suggests that the best way for classical drama to be staged is with men playing the female roles, thereby highlighting their status as "classic drag" and countering inclinations to take their misogynist stereotypes as realistic representations of women (Case 1988: 15). These arguments put feminists at the RSC in an impossible position, asking them to disavow either their company or their politics.

Of course, not all of the actors at the RSC were interested in feminist theatre or feminist politics. Although their label as the "RSC Women's Group" implied that all the women at the RSC were involved and united, the group members had little in common other than their presence at the RSC. There was only a small number of women who were engaged with feminism; others joined the meetings because they saw an opportunity for work or because they were curious about what was going on. Still others were not interested and did not participate. The tensions among the Women's Group members were not insignificant, according to recollections of their meetings. Hands heard that there was a lot of discord after he left his initial discussion with the women. Shaw says that "there was a group that was very anti- the group, but who were in it anyway," and Stevenson describes the group's diffuseness as disabling: "We sat around as a group of actresses who had not chosen to be together, who had not selected each other because we were like-minded, because we shared an ideal or a dream or a vision. . . . Most of the time we were functioning there was fear, mistrust, frustration, ambitiousness" (Woddis 1987: 14). The creation of the "RSC Women's Group" was more convenient for separating their project from the rest of the RSC's work than for identifying a particular political or theatrical practice. The label did succeed, however, in reinforcing women's secondary status within the company by semantically reminding participants and observers that women were contained by but separate from the neutral RSC. As Victoria Radin quips in the *New Statesman* review of the group's final project:

> If the plays in the repertory of the Royal Shakespeare Company were labelled [*sic*] in terms of the gender of their directors, they would all of them be designated "men's projects". I mention this because the play I am about to discuss grew out of, and has been designated, "the women's project" – conferring on half the population the special minority status of a group of visiting Martians.
>
> (Radin 1987)

Ultimately, this "special minority status" was more important in defining the Women's Group than any coherent political identity.

The Women's Group did have one small bit of common ground: they wanted to work, in Todd's words, on "an epic or mythic canvas." Out of this interest in doing something that "broke out of the constraints of naturalism," Todd went to see Angela Carter, who had reworked a series of fairy tales for her 1979 story collection *The Bloody Chamber*. Todd described the Women's Group to Carter and then asked her advice about an appropriate piece. Her response, as Todd remembers, was, "It's a bloody place for doing bloody Shakespeare. You want to do Shakespeare. Do *Macbeth*." Carter's logic was that in an institution that did Shakespeare, women should take control of the text and make it their own; she felt in particular that *Macbeth* was a taboo play for women with its vision of patricide, and as such would offer the group a chance for a feminist intervention into the cultural production of Shakespeare. Certainly much of the play's horror depends on images of monstrous motherhood. Lady Macbeth begs the spirits to "unsex me here" and to "Come to my woman's breasts, / And take my milk for gall" (1.5.39, 45–6); more horrific is her threat of infanticide:

> I have given suck, and know
> How tender 'tis to love the babe that milks me.
> I would, while it was smiling in my face,
> Have plucked my nipple from his boneless gums
> And dashed the brains out, had I so sworn
> As you have done to this.
>
> (1.7.54–9)

These images of the murderous mother make Lady Macbeth a complicated heroine. On the one hand, she appears to be a travesty of all things women are supposed to be – a mother willing to kill her child, a daughter who calls for the murder of her figurative father. On the other, she anticipates the role of the perfect modern wife, supportive of her husband and keeper of domestic space. As Phyllis Rackin points out, the Scottish wives of Holinshed's *Chronicles* leave their castles to fight alongside their husbands, while Lady Macbeth remains resolutely in the castle, and Renaissance noblewomen used wetnurses rather than breastfeed their children as Lady Macbeth describes having done (Rackin 1998: 33–5). If Lady Macbeth was thus an anomaly in her own time, her character has continued to present challenges to later centuries' notions of womanhood. Examining Victorian pictorial representations of Lady Macbeth, Georgianna Ziegler argues that "These two images of Lady Macbeth – as barbaric and passionate or domesticated and caring – figure the conflicted notions about women's roles in the nineteenth century" (Ziegler 1999: 137). Turning to media depictions of Hillary Rodham Clinton, Ziegler finds that these conflicting notions extend to our own time, "figur[ing] our society's conflicted admiration for and fear of women's rights, power, and professional success" (Ziegler 1999: 138). That the play resonates so clearly with questions about women's roles suggests that *Macbeth* had the potential to be a perfect vehicle for the Women's Group's explorations.

When Todd went to Terry Hands, however, he rejected an all-female *Macbeth* outright. Todd recalls that "Terry just went, 'Well, no. We, I mean, no. I, well, we, no. No, definitely not,'" and that he did not offer a good reason for his refusal, aside from his insistence that the group should do a new piece. Todd is not sure what his objection was, offering that it is possible that Hands rejected the idea because it was not substantial enough, or that she did not make a strong proposal, or that he "just didn't want a bunch of women doing Shakespeare." According to Genista McIntosh, Hands' objections to the piece were grounded in RSC notions about what is appropriate for Shakespeare:

> The objections that were raised by Terry were firstly, that it wasn't a very good idea anyway. But also that it was one of the popular plays, and we didn't give those plays to people who were sort of first-time directors. So there was a whole RSC ideology/mythology about how you do the plays of Shakespeare that came into play the minute they said, "The thing we want to do, is what you do, boys." And the boys went, "Oh no, we didn't mean *that*; we didn't mean that, we meant do something girly."

Hands himself does not remember any suggestion of working on *Macbeth*, although he says now that it could have been a good idea to use Shakespeare as source material for a new project. He does add that *Macbeth* itself might have been a difficult play for the group to work on, since it is Macbeth himself who drives much of the action of the play; he rejects the idea of an all-female version as "silly."

Although it might be true that Hands strongly felt the group should present a new work, that does not contradict McIntosh's assessment of his response. The RSC ideology of how to do Shakespeare stemmed from artistic concerns about creating a "house style" for the company, but was more immediately a consequence of their financial worries about staying solvent. The RSC faced continual money problems throughout the 1980s (leading eventually to the company's structural overhaul in the late 1990s). Its subsidies from the Arts Council and other sources fell from covering 44 per cent of their total costs in the 1984/5 season to 36 per cent in the 1986/7 season. Meanwhile, its paid admissions fell from 894,654 in their Stratford and London theatres to 827,415 – the decline was even more dramatic than these numbers suggest, as the Swan's debut in November 1986 hid the large drop in attendance at the Barbican that year (Royal Shakespeare Company 1987b). To stem financial decline, the company needed substantially to increase ticket sales, even while continually appealing to the government to raise its subsidy. With growing competition for money and audiences from the National Theatre and other classical theatre companies, the RSC began to position itself more forcefully in the commercial market, relying particularly on West End- or Broadway-style shows, such as their productions of *Nicholas Nickleby*, *Les Miserables* and *Kiss Me Kate* (see Mullin 1994: xxii–xxiii for a very brief overview of these circumstances). The commercialization of the RSC also entailed a greater reliance on the most popular of Shakespeare's plays. Recycling plays is a problem Shakespeare companies always face – the same ones get chosen time and again (see Taylor 1999a: 347 and Holland 1997: 7–10). But in a climate of dwindling resources and audiences, the most popular plays become all the more important. In the spring of 1986, when Todd proposed doing *Macbeth* (one of the big four tragedies and a set text for school exams), the company could not risk having it fall short as a money-maker. The administration's sense of what was marketable Shakespeare meant that the play had to be reserved for a more classical and serious treatment than could be entrusted to what was perceived as a bunch of women with little experience. The play was, in fact, directed by Adrian Noble for the 1986/7 Stratford season.[10]

After Hands' negative response to their *Macbeth* proposal, the Women's Group realized that, in McIntosh's words, "the only way they were going to get it [their project] past first base was by coming up with something that wasn't going to be threatening in any area to anybody else's territory." But while a non-threatening "girly" production would create opportunities for women to work, it would fail to challenge the RSC's preconceptions about the value of female work. The separation of the Women's Group from the company's main purpose had the effect of suggesting not just that women do theatre other than Shakespeare, but that they cannot do Shakespeare. When the Women's Group came back to Hands with something completely removed from the realm of classical theatre, they became "girly" at the expense of making Shakespeare a legitimate arena for women's work. Shortly after the failure of the *Macbeth* idea, the main instigators behind the group's formation pulled out of their planned project. Todd had put together a proposal that did not tread on any RSC toes: a staged version of the Cinderella myth written by Timberlake Wertenbaker in collaboration with Marina Warner. But when Wertenbaker learned that neither Shaw nor Stevenson had promised to participate, she refused to proceed, according to Todd: "[she] said quite rightly, 'Well if they're not prepared to commit themselves, nor am I.'"[11] Todd went to both Shaw and Stevenson to try to convince them to continue with the project, but had no success: "I remember going to have a long talk with Fiona about doing this Cinderella project, and she was charming and slippery, and wouldn't commit herself, basically. Interested, but she wouldn't commit herself." As for Stevenson,

> Juliet wept and stormed and wept and said, "I have to leave the RSC, I can't stand it any longer, it's just killing me, I can't bear it." She felt the place was just consuming her and that even for a women's project she was not prepared to stick it out.

When asked about it now, Shaw explains that she left the group when she was offered the RSC national tour (playing Beatrice in *Much Ado About Nothing* and Portia in *Merchant of Venice*), because she wanted to get out of London and to concentrate on classical roles. McIntosh, however, suggests that she and Stevenson left the group once it became apparent that its revolutionary potential had faded:

> I suspect that in both their cases, and in the others who dropped away, it was that it was fun while there was a real possibility that you could have got into the inner sanctum. And when they began to see that actually they were still outside the walls and were being thrown a crumb, it didn't seem worth doing to them.

Although Shaw does not say so explicitly, she seems to hint that she might have been dissatisfied with the group's lack of revolutionary power, not in terms of what the administration was offering them, but rather in the way some of the women involved with the group did not share her feminist values. Certainly personnel conflicts played a large role in the group's problems. Todd says that she believes that Shaw and Stevenson did not want to commit to the project because they wanted to keep their career options open. But she wonders if perhaps Shaw in particular might have thought, "Well, I can see this might be a disaster, or I might have to work with X, whom I can't stand." She also thinks it is possible that they left because they regretted having asked her to direct the project. Having been invited into the group, Todd quickly took charge, getting down to the ruthless business of settling on a piece, finding the resources and casting the right actors. She admits that she "made a fuss" and that they might have "found that alienating." It is also possible that Todd's own desire to keep her career options open fueled some problems. There were suggestions that Todd was more interested in her own power and status than in the group's overall success: she had always wanted to be a director for the RSC, claims this line of argument, and saw the group as potentially a path to further engagements with the company. Todd herself, while admitting that she felt she deserved a piece of this pie, denies that she had been angling for a long-term role in the RSC. Hands counters that even if it were true, it is not such a bad thing; freelance directors are dependent on creating good productions in order to generate future work. Regardless of the various reasons for members' departures and for tensions between the remaining participants, it is clear that financial and career pressures are impossible to separate from the group's fate.

By this point (June 1986) it was becoming crucial that the group start work on something in order for it to be ready by December. There was pressure to come up with a title to put in the new brochures, and planning meetings were already underway to allocate resources for the new season. But according to Todd, "nobody [from the group] came with a lively idea." Todd herself was becoming increasingly frustrated and unhappy with the group, finding their meetings "grim" and "point-less" and feeling that "it was going to be a miserable undertaking." She went to Hands on a few occasions and said she no longer wanted to do this, but he urged her to stick with it. Finally Todd thought, "I have one more card to play" – her relationship with playwright Deborah Levy, with whom she had worked in the Women's Theatre Group in 1985. Todd proposed to Levy that her newest piece be adapted for the Women's Group, and so *Heresies* became their project. Once the play was set, Todd began to finalize cast details. Many of the women from the early group meetings had either left, like Shaw and Stevenson, or their contracts had not been renewed when the RSC went through its major personnel shift between seasons. Of the women who had been in Stratford for the group's gestation, only Susan Colverd and Penelope Freeman remained for the London project. Caroline Goodall, Miriam Karlin, Tina Marian and Susan Tracy joined the RSC for new produc-tions and subsequently joined the group. Todd brought in the rest of the cast herself: Paola Dionisotti, Ann Mitchell, Roger Allam and Clive Russell were Monstrous Regiment associates; Nimmy March was a students of Todd's at Guildhall; and Stella Gonet was someone whose work Todd had admired. Todd also brought in another former associ-ate, Iona McLeish, as the designer. In the end, *Heresies* was more of an outside production than something that emerged from within the RSC.

Neither the rehearsal period nor the final production of *Heresies* was well received by the RSC actors or reviewers. Todd insisted on a series of collaborative workshops to develop the play, a process with which most of the actors felt uncomfortable. The weeks of preparation also led to trouble when it came time to edit the script; although both Levy and Todd felt that the play needed to be cut and reshaped, the actors refused to give up any of their lines. The final production revolved around twelve characters and a plethora of themes about displacement, loss, refugees, business, art, politics and family. It was, true to Todd's wishes, not a naturalistic drama: the characters were representative types (such as the Displaced Person, the Courtesan, the Lonely Businessman) as well as individuals, and the language they spoke was poetic and highly expressionistic. Confronted with such unusual fare for mainstream theatre, the play's reviewers complained that it was messy, more concerned with ideas than realistic characters and dialogue. That *Heresies* was the product of a group of women was repeatedly made fun of, as in Milton Shulman's review for the *Evening Standard*: "Whatever else may be said about *Heresies* at The Pit, it cannot be blamed on a man" and "the result is not so much a pseud's corner as a pseud's kitchen, in which naive feminist notions are brewed and half-baked" (Shulman 1986). Whatever the ambitions of the Women's Group in its early days, they were never realized. With the end of the *Heresies* run, the group disbanded – it had really ceased to exist from the moment the play was cast, since the majority of participants had not been part of its visionary origins. By the time of the production, the Women's Group had become simply a name for the women doing a one-time project; although the statement in the program notes pointed to hopes for future productions, it seems that few of them envisaged such a thing.

In the end, it is the distance between the Women's Group's initial formation and its final project that offers the best lessons about the place of women in the Royal Shakespeare Company. There was clearly, in 1985, a discontent among many of the company's women that reflected serious problems both within the RSC and with its reputation. All was not well in the company. Brigid Larmour, an assistant director at the RSC from 1982 to 1985, was very frustrated that none of the female assistant directors there with her were allowed to move up in the company ranks. She was, however, unable to remedy the situation:

> I put a proposal together which involved Di Trevis, Annie Castledine and myself taking over The Other Place, which both Terry Hands and Trevor Nunn said was a terribly interesting proposal and that they'd set up a meeting when they were both free, and this went on for months and months and months – and nothing ever happened.
>
> (Manfull 1997: 16, 180)

Trevis was given the 1985/6 tour to direct, but neither Larmour nor Castledine were given their own productions at the RSC. Clearly Stevenson and Shaw weren't the only ones to note the lack of opportunities for women to advance in the company.

From that era of discontent, however, little seems to have emerged at the RSC. There is certainly still a dearth of female administrators at the company. Genista McIntosh left as Senior Administrator in 1990, joining the National Theatre as Executive Director. As she points out, more than ten years after the Women's Group, "there are still no women at the top of the organization": the administrative staff is over-whelmingly male, and, with the exception of Katie Mitchell's brief tenure as Artistic Director of The Other Place, the senior artistic man-agement is entirely male. The one significant area of change has been an increase in the number of women directing at the company. Since 1986, almost a dozen women have directed productions; before then there had been only seven.[12] The majority of these women, however, have not directed Shakespeare. Since 1986, only Di Trevis, Deborah Warner, Cicely Berry, Gale Edwards and Katie Mitchell have directed productions of his plays, and only Trevis and Edwards have been allowed on the company's main stage, the Royal Shakespeare Theatre; only Edwards has directed Shakespeare at the Barbican Theatre, the company's main stage in London.

Although most of these women have directed a wide range of non-Shakespearean drama at the company, from medieval mysteries to Jacobean tragedies to Chekhov, the breadth of their Shakespeare offer-ings is strikingly limited. Trevis and Edwards were both asked to direct comedies (both were in fact given *The Taming of the Shrew*, although Trevis went on to direct *Much Ado About Nothing* on the main stage in 1988). Warner has directed a couple of the tragedies, but only minor and relatively unpopular ones (*Titus Andronicus* in 1987 and *King John* in 1988; this is not to diminish the huge success of her *Titus*, which con-tinues to be praised and has been canonized in academic studies of the play). Katie Mitchell directed *3 Henry VI* for The Other Place and the national tour in 1994. This is regarded as one of the most minor of Shakespeare's history plays, and had never been performed on its own in Stratford before Mitchell's production. Cicely Berry is the only one to have been allowed to direct a major tragedy, *King Lear*, in 1989, but this was an educational project designed primarily for school groups. It played only brief runs in The Other Place and at the Almeida Theatre in London (once the RSC's London base, but superseded by the Barbican in the early 1980s). Her production, as well being outside the RSC's regular season, was clearly marked off as being directed by the company's voice coach, implying that Berry's direction was more an extension of her regular voice work than a full directorial intervention. Despite the increased presence of women directing at the RSC, there is still clearly a perception that major productions of Shakespeare cannot be entrusted to their care.

It is unlikely that it would ever have been possible for the Women's Group to change anything at the RSC. Even aside from the tensions within the group and the disagreements about politics, the structure of the group and its relationship to the RSC precluded any serious revolutionary potential. As made evident by its name, the RSC Women's Group was completely contained within the RSC. If the women wanted to punch Daddy, as Shaw suggests, Daddy was never going to give them the tools actually to unseat him. Todd now doubts there was ever any serious intention to alter the RSC's gender politics: "I don't think Terry or any of the dominant RSC voices, including Genista McIntosh at that time, had any notion of including women in the organization in a way that mattered creatively." McIntosh herself agrees that it was never really possible that the Women's Group would get what they wanted:

> It was an unequal struggle. They wanted Terry to say, "I give in." And he was never going to. And so a tremendous amount of energy went into trying to achieve something that actually wasn't achievable. Whatever kind of capitulation in some way they felt it was possible to achieve, really it just wasn't going to happen. And the mark that has been left by that is so faint, that even I can barely discern it.

It is easy to look back at the group and say they went about things the wrong way: they should have addressed those structural factors at the RSC which stymied women's advancement, they should have worked more closely with the female assistant directors who were already there, they should have insisted on doing a project about Shakespeare. But this sort of hindsight ignores the more insidious ways in which the RSC was resistant to change. It was not just the specific details or the larger artistic and management philosophies that kept women out; it was the company's inability to confess its own complicity with the status quo. In a May 1986 interview, RSC literary manager Colin Chambers spoke about the different responses of company administrators to the question of how to include more women:

> We have discussed and do discuss quite often how should the company overcome its clear bias. And then you get caught up in this argument to do with positive discrimination as against something supposedly called quality. . . . There are roughly two positions inside the company. . . . One is that we must in some way encourage

women to be represented, but that they must go through exactly the same process of selection or competition or whatever as everybody else, i.e., the men. The other is that this very process is precisely the process that excludes them. And that you have got to do something much more radical and actually interventionist, and that is a much bigger risk.

(Carlson 1991: 332)

The choices the company set for itself here – leave things the same or engage in risky, radical interventions – were really no choice at all. The opposition they created was a weighted one between the normal (being predominantly male) and the radical (having sexual equality). In a large, nationally subsidized theatre company trying to contain its financial losses, the alignment of women with risk makes the move towards gender parity unthinkable. By the mid-1990s, when the wider theatrical community began to feel itself at risk (and when the rise of Labour failed to produce more generous funding for the arts), the feasibility of female directors and administrators began to take on different associations.[13] But in the mid-1980s, the RSC was reluctant to make anything but the easiest and most superficial changes. The company could point to Di Trevis as an example of a woman rising through the ranks, and to Deborah Warner to show its willingness to hire new female faces. Questions about more systematic changes, however, went unanswered. The inertia of such a large body as the Royal Shakespeare Company, particularly during the period both of its greatest number of productions and its greatest financial losses, would take more to overcome it than one briefly active women's group, cut short by internal divisions and a lack of firm mandates.

3

The Taming of the Shrew
A case study in performance criticism

The process of writing about performed Shakespeare is never a straightforward one. The text is the usual place to begin: what is a playscript about and what issues raised in the script must be addressed in a performance? But such a starting-point assumes that there is an agreed script and that there are agreed elements in the script to be addressed. Certainly a history of performances of the play offers another place to begin locating the resonant elements of a script: how have other performers dealt with the play? But, in considering performance history, one must also address the various material factors that affect the performances: what sort of theatres were used and what sort of audiences attended those theatres? While all of these elements need to be worked through in setting up a specific production of a Shakespeare play, there are as many factors to be considered in evaluating the production. There is the question of the reviews to address: who wrote reviews for this production, what were their criteria for evaluation, what ideologies are reflected in their criteria, for whom were they writing? One's own response to a performance is no less complicated: what is the difference between watching a performance and recalling a performance, and why do different viewers see and recall different things? How, finally, does one work with all of these questions and bring them together in an act of criticism about performed Shakespeare?

This chapter takes my own experience of working with Gale

Edwards' 1995 RSC production of *The Taming of the Shrew* as a case study in the process of writing performance criticism. Both Edwards and *Shrew* allow me to examine further a mixture of gender politics and performances of Shakespeare. This production also highlights many of the issues that arose in earlier chapters about actor training and women at the RSC. The chapter is divided into sections along the lines of my initial questions: textual and performance history, production analysis, reviewer response, critical interpretation. Each section is self-contained, but, as the chapter progresses, the divisions break down in important ways. Although the opening of the chapter does not rely on a personal narrative, as I begin to work with Edwards' production and with its reviews, the personal plays an unavoidable role. One of the persistent myths of scholarship, despite the body of theory that tries to counter it, is that we can objectively scrutinize our subjects. As this chapter reveals, the role of the personal is a crucial element in working with performed Shakespeare, a factor that is impossible to separate from the seemingly discrete status of "the text" and "the production." And ultimately, the more carefully one works through a critical reading of performed Shakespeare, the less likely it is that the performance will appear to assert the Bard's universality.

Working with the text on page and stage

The Taming of the Shrew is a particularly apt play through which to examine feminist performances. It is, of course, notorious for its misogyny: the story of a bachelor who vows to "wive it wealthily" (1.2.72), marries a shrew who will listen to no man, and tames her through starvation, threatened violence and mental anguish until she submits to him absolutely. This plot line makes clear the problems any reader or viewer, particularly a feminist one, might have. But for someone wishing to disrupt its patriarchal thrust, the structure of the play itself creates problems. Despite the fact that it is Katherine who shifts from being an unmarried shrew to a submissive wife, the play is more the story of Petruchio, her tamer. She gets fewer lines than him, no soliloquies, few asides and little or no chance to explain her apparent change in temperament. Paola Dionisotti, who played Katherine in Michael Bogdanov's 1978 RSC production, describes the dilemma:

> I wanted the play to be about Kate and about a woman instinctively fighting sexism. But I don't really think that's what the play is about. It's not the story of Kate: it's the story of Petruchio. He gets the

soliloquies, he gets the moments of change. All the crucial moments
of the story for Kate, she's off stage.

(Rutter 1989: 1)

Although Katherine is on stage for about a third of the play, she speaks
for only a third of that third. Petruchio is the one whose words dominate. He speaks significantly more than any of the other characters, with
158 speeches and 584 lines – 17.7 per cent of the total number of
speeches in the play and 21.8 per cent of its lines (Spevack 1968: 994).
Katherine, on the other hand, has 82 speeches, or 9.2 per cent, and
219 lines, or 8.2 per cent (Spevack 1968: 979); she speaks more
than Hortensio, who has 7.8 per cent of the lines spoken, but less
than Tranio, who at 11.0 per cent of lines spoken comes the clos-
est to achieving Petruchio's logorrhea (Spevack 1968: 974, 1007).
Katherine's one big moment, the only time in which she is unequivocally center stage, is her submission speech. She takes the stage with the
longest speech of the play only to mark her removal from it and, after
those forty-four lines, never speaks again.[1]

It is perhaps Katherine's absent motivation that makes the play's
ending so difficult to fathom as either possible or desirable. This skepticism is not rooted in modern feminism alone. Shakespeare's *Shrew* is
the only one of his plays that triggered a response from another
Renaissance playwright – something that suggests both the controversy
surrounding the play and the consternation at its conclusion. John
Fletcher's *The Woman's Prize, or The Tamer Tamed* (circa 1611) tells *Shrew*'s
sequel in which, after Katherine's death, Petruchio is tamed by his
second wife, Maria. Fletcher's play can be read as expressing skepticism
about both the success of Petruchio's taming method (it is repeatedly
implied that he is only tamed by Maria because he is so exhausted from
his struggles with Katherine) and the desirability of Katherine's submission (Fletcher's epilogue declares that his play's purpose is "To teach
both Sexes due equality; / And as they stand bound, to love mutually"
(Epi. 7–8)). Ann Thompson points out that Fletcher's play situates
Shakespeare's as part of a common debate about the war between
the sexes in which a tale of a woman's submission is paired with a
tale of a man's submission (Thompson 1984: 18). Similar exchanges
can be found in Chaucer's *Canterbury Tales* and in the Renaissance
pamphlet wars. On at least one occasion, the two plays were performed
as a sequence during the early modern period. Sir Henry Herbert
records that when Shakespeare's *Shrew* was performed at the court of
Charles I in 1633, it was "liked"; when Fletcher's *The Woman's Prize* was

performed a few days later, it was "very well liked" (Oliver 1982: 64). H. J. Oliver, the editor of the Oxford edition of Shakespeare's play, interprets Herbert's record as evidence of the court's poor literary judgement. Another reaction would be to focus on ideology rather than aesthetics, and to recognize that the court's judgment might be a response to the forms of patriarchy jockeying for position in the plays. Perhaps that audience liked the misogynist's comeuppance better than his earlier triumph. The growing influence of the Protestant ideal of companionate marriage may have led to a shift in preference from a play valuing submission over affection to a play that calls for equality and mutual love. Whatever the reason, this momentary triumph of Fletcher's play belies the notion of a stable and universally acceptable Renaissance patriarchy. As Leah Marcus notes, "Patriarchy as a system has regularly been more consistent and orderly in the minds of histor-ically inclined editors and readers than it has been in society at large" (Marcus 1996: 129). The possibility that Renaissance viewers preferred Fletcher's inversion of Shakespeare's taming story suggests that early modern attitudes towards *Shrew* were not as monolithic as some of the play's later readers would like to believe.

If Renaissance reactions to *Shrew* are not monolithic, neither is the Renaissance text. The ideological split we see between Shakespeare's and Fletcher's plays can also be seen in the contested textual history of *The Taming of the Shrew* and its relationship to the 1594 quarto, *The Taming of a Shrew*. *A Shrew*, as it has come to be differentiated from the 1623 Folio *The Shrew*, presents a very different version of the story we now know as Shakespeare's. In *A Shrew*, the Sly-frame (which appears only at the beginning of *The Shrew*) asserts its presence throughout the play, serving both to remind us of the taming story's metatheatrical nature (it is a story told within the story of Sly's gulling) and to under-cut the success of the taming. Within the frame story there are also differences that complicate the taming, including the addition of asides for Katherine and changes to her final speech. For at least some Renaissance readers of the quarto, its hero's success in controlling his wife was not convincing. John Harington's 1596 *The Metamorphosis of Ajax* records his skepticism: "For the shrewd wife, read the booke of taming a shrew, which hath made a number of us so perfect, that now every one can rule a shrew in our countrey, save he that hath her" (Oliver 1982: 34). Harington's reaction implies that Katherine's dutiful submission remains contained within the frame as a moment of wish-fulfillment, never to be achieved by Sly or any other husband. With the complete Sly-framework, argues Marcus, "Shrew-taming becomes the compensatory fantasy of a socially underprivileged male" (Marcus 1996: 104) and not the culturally desirable and realistic goal it appears to be in *The Shrew*. Modern readers and editors debate whether or not *The Shrew* is more or less oppressively patriarchal than *A Shrew*, and what the exact relationship is between the two plays, with most agreeing that *The Shrew* is decidedly less offensive than *A Shrew* and that *A Shrew* should not be attributed to Shakespeare. However, Marcus argues astutely both that *A Shrew* is less oppressive and that modern editors' desire unequivocally to separate the two texts comes from their own wish to tame the unruly feminine quarto (Marcus 1996: 101–31). Comparison with *A Shrew*, as with *The Woman's Prize*, reveals Shakespeare's play to be a source of continual debate.

Subsequent treatment of the play on stage continues to display unease with its gender politics. In her introduction to the Cambridge edition of the play, Ann Thompson asserts that *Shrew* "has probably been played straight less often than any other play in the canon" (Thompson 1984: 18). From the mid-1660s until 1764, John Lacey's *Sauny the Scott, or The Taming of the Shrew* reigned the stage; from 1764 until the middle of the nineteenth century, David Garrick's *Catharine and Petruchio* was the preferred version of Shakespeare's play. Both versions simultaneously exaggerate the play's violence (Lacey's hero sends for a surgeon to pull his wife's teeth out and Garrick's wielded a whip) and seek to soften it (both substantially cut the final submission speech, the actor playing Lacey's heroine is given an epilogue in which she explicitly distances herself from such a tame and "unwomanly" submission, and Garrick's Petruchio concludes the submission speech himself). The appeal of these versions, which successfully replaced Shakespeare's *Shrew* on stage for two hundred years, indicates their era's general preference for rewritten Shakespeare. More importantly, it exposes a discomfort with the play's gender politics. Both Lacey and Garrick – and their cultures – endorse the idea of a husband's superiority, but their exaggerations and qualifications suggest a sense that Shakespeare's play has gone too far in its masculinist ideology. Shakespeare's full text was not returned to the stage until 1844 in London and 1887 in New York – the last of his plays to be so restored.[2]

The "restoration" of Shakespeare's text did not diminish the play's capacity to reflect contemporary gender anxieties. Both sides of the debate over the women's suffrage movement used the play to support their stance. During the 1909 Shakespeare Festival in Stratford-upon-Avon, an important by-election focused attention on the issue of women's voting rights. Political speeches and rallies were held in town during the Festival, which itself culminated in Frank and Catherine Benson's performance of *Shrew*. Susan Carlson argues persuasively that this production of *Shrew* was a reflection of and contribution to the debate and was understood by its participants and audience as playing an active role in the question of suffrage (Carlson 1998). More than two decades later, a 1933 article in the *East Anglian Times* wished that the play had succeeded in taming the activists:

> That *The Taming* was presented [at Stratford] for eight years in succession from 1909 onwards may perhaps be accounted for in some measure as being due to the activities of the vote-hungry viragoes who from 1910 to the eve of the War were breaking windows, setting fire to churches, chaining themselves to railings, and generally demonstrating their fitness to be endowed with Parliamentary responsibility. Katherina's "purple patch" concerning the duty of women . . . was a smashing rejoinder to the militant Furies who were making fools of themselves in the ways indicated.
>
> (Thompson 1984: 21–2)

But as Carlson points out, those "militant Furies" often saw Katherine as an emblem for their cause; "In those early years of the twentieth century, *The Shrew* served both as a balm to salve the wounds opened up by activist women threatening most of the political and cultural institutions of their day and also as a rallying cry for those who made Shakespeare preeminent among the suffragists" (Carlson 1998: 96). As in earlier years, the meaning of the play was never completely stable. Indeed, its long history of rewrites and controversies suggests that revision might be more natural to *The Taming of the Shrew* than a deceptively faithful enactment.[3]

Looking for Katherine

In an effort to understand both the play and its heroine, many early feminist scholars approached *The Taming of the Shrew* by trying to look at it from Katherine's viewpoint. Often their work claimed that she fell in love with Petruchio and that her final "submission" speech was part of a mutual game between the two. Carol Thomas Neely saw a Katherine who, by experiencing love for the first time, matured from shrew to woman: "her ability to combine assertion and accommodation and her newfound pleasure in giving and receiving affection are confirmed in her final speech, a celebration of reciprocity" (Neely 1985: 30). By focusing on Katherine rather than Petruchio, scholars strove to make her the central character and to make the play something other than repugnant. As Neely admits, her reading "has the effect of taming the taming" (Neely 1985: 218). But in looking for Katherine's story, scholars were often driven by their own stories. In a long and oft-quoted footnote, Neely locates her argument alongside those made by other feminists and finds that they are

> responding, sometimes explicitly, to conflicting impulses – to their profound abhorrence of male dominance and female submission and to their equally profound pleasure at the play's conclusion, a pleasure created by the comic movement of the whole. Both impulses must be acknowledged. Feminists cannot, without ignoring altogether the play's meaning and structure, fail to rejoice at the spirit, wit, and joy with which Kate accommodates herself to her wifely role. Within the world of the play there are no preferable alternatives. But we cannot fail to note the radical asymmetry and inequality of the comic reconciliation and wish for Kate, as for ourselves, accommodations more mutual and less coerced.
>
> (Neely 1985: 218–19)

For this first wave of feminist Shakespeare scholars, intent on recuperating the hidden stories of plays neglected by generations of male critics, *Shrew* was caught up in their desire to rewrite Shakespeare as the loving, supportive father that their own institutions had too often failed to be. Katherine's accommodation to an unfair world mirrored their own.

Other feminists, of course, saw a different story, one that emphasized the taming's violence. But regardless of whether one chooses to see Katherine as a spirited wife or a battered woman, the desire to find her point of view is a powerful urge for readers of the play. Given *Shrew*'s unpalatable ideology and the lack of a textual explanation for Katherine's transformation from shrew to docile wife, feminists are drawn to look outside the text in order to understand what they see within. If Katherine is not given the words to explain her change in character, we must supply them ourselves. In this way, *Shrew*'s notorious gender politics focus attention on the interaction between text and audience; readers and viewers must choose how to align themselves to the play and how to interpret its characters. As both Lynda Boose and Barbara Hodgdon argue, Katherine's final speech in particular depends upon this transaction between audience and text. Asked by Petruchio to "tell these headstrong women / What duty they do owe their lords and husbands" (5.2.134–5), Katherine's speech praising the obedience of wives is addressed specifically to the women on stage, but also to those in the off-stage audience. In Boose's words,

> Kate's final *pièce de non résistance* is constructed not as the speech of a discrete character speaking her role within the expressly marked-out boundaries of a play frame; it is a textual moment in which, in Althusserian terms, the play quite overtly "interpellates," or hails, its women viewers into an imaginary relationship with the ideology of the discourse being played out onstage by their counterparts.
>
> (Boose 1991: 180)

According to Hodgdon, Katherine's character is never discrete, but always shifting according to the demands of the audience: "How Kate's subjectivity is constructed is always monitored and adjusted by the perceptions and desires of consuming subjects whose complex histories and multiple cultural affiliations exceed those of the textual subject" (Hodgdon 1998: 2). Crucially, for a consideration of feminist performances, she claims that this unstable subjectivity can be a source of pleasure: "Perhaps the play's most compelling attraction lies less in its ability to determine gender difference absolutely than in the contradictions it engenders between Kate's seemingly circumscribed position and its openness to the phantasmatic scenarios viewers bring to it" (Hodgdon 1998: 2). The very qualities that make *Shrew* a problem play – its underwritten characterizations and repressive ideology – can also be the source of subversive pleasure for feminists, one that counters the authoritative pleasure that comes from aligning oneself with the traditionally universal Shakespeare.[4]

Interpreting the unwritten, however, is no easy matter. It might be tempting to exchange one point of view for another – reworking Shakespearean gender ideology by speaking through his female characters rather than the male, telling Katherine's story instead of Petruchio's. However, this replacement fails to acknowledge the pervasiveness of the text's ideology. Boose claims that critiquing *Shrew* from within the text in this manner will inevitably be a limited strategy, producing readings that "are virtually incapable of emancipating either female or male readers from the relentlessly gendered experience that the dynamics of this play have constituted as inseparable from its fulfillment of comic desire" (Boose 1994: 194). Her argument relies in part on a notion of characterization similar to that proposed by Alan Sinfield, who argues that it involves a dramaturgical strategy that may be invoked or abandoned as needed (Sinfield 1991: 52–79). In Boose's reading, Katherine does not have her own story which can be told separately from that of the play; she is a character in a playscript designed to fulfill patriarchal functions, and reading for "her story" simply hides the way in which it is designed to be a story of masculine domination. Substituting your subjectivity for Katherine's will never make the play change. Boose's way around this dilemma is to tease out the strands that make up the story told by the play. She locates *Shrew* in its Renaissance culture, examining how that culture's material conditions help to create a play invested in "the reinstatement of a hierarchically gendered order" (Boose 1994: 196). Her scholarship reveals the historical context of land enclosure debates that put ideological pressure on the play, suggesting that class tensions about land use were displaced onto the gender struggle between Katherine and Petruchio. In this reading, Katherine's final capitulation has to do less with her psychological journey than with a nostalgic need for order. Boose succeeds in her feminist criticism by filling in the gaps of the story with history, not with character. Seen another way, she uncovers the construction of Katherine's character instead of the character itself.[5]

While Boose is able to preserve Katherine's radically unstable character in her scholarship, productions of *Shrew* are faced with a different set of demands. There is not, in performance, a context of historical documents against which to read the playscript, but a group of embodied characters who look like people with individual histories. Although programs and other materials might try to provide a contextual background for the play, audiences of Shakespeare – even more so than those of other dramas – respond to the play primarily through the persons on stage. Because we value Shakespeare as our progenitor, and because we think of actors as bringing written characters to life, we regard his staged characters as people – fictional, yes, but also organized like ourselves, with stories and feelings that we can identify. Katherine, no matter what the history of enclosure or theories of subjectivity reveal, has a personal story to tell up on stage. It is in her story that Hodgdon locates the play's subversive pleasure, the excitement of constituting her character the way we want to. But it is also in her story that the play's danger lies, the risk that audiences will read it in a way that validates their own potentially patriarchal desires.

Setting up contexts: the "*Shrew* option" and the Royal Shakespeare Theatre

In 1995, Gale Edwards directed *The Taming of the Shrew* for the Royal Shakespeare Company on their main stage in Stratford-upon-Avon.

While this production marked the company's fifth *Shrew* in thirteen years and the second by a woman, it also marked only the third time a woman had directed in the Royal Shakespeare Theatre.[6] The low frequency of women directing on the main stage and relativity high frequency of women directing *Shrew* creates some interesting contexts for Edwards' production. The absence of female directors at the RST follows the pattern of male Shakespeare that I have traced in the previous chapters. But what does it mean that this play seems to be marked at the RSC as more female than others? The "*Shrew* option," as director Susan Lily Todd calls the practise of hiring women to direct this play, acknowledges and circumvents the play's notorious misogyny. The playscript centers on silencing a woman and climaxes with making her the mouthpiece for a nostalgic and regressive notion of women's duty to prostrate themselves before their husbands.[7] By inviting a female director to be the voice behind the mouthpiece, a predominantly male company can distance itself from the suggestion that women need to be made to obey their male lords. But if this move places female directors in the position of Shakespeare (the authorial director substituting for the authorial playwright), it also places them in the position of Katherine, authorized to proclaim the inferiority of women. Having a woman direct *The Taming of the Shrew*, in other words, sets up oppositional ideologies: the female director's presence legitimizes women's interpretations of Shakespeare, while the playscript's patriarchal thrust silences women.

Staging the production in the main theatre of the company creates additional tensions. The audience for the RSC's base in Stratford is largely made up of tourists, particularly overseas tourists who come to see Shakespeare performed in the town of his birth. Another portion of the audience is school parties taken to see Shakespeare as part of their studies. Both of these groups expect to see productions of the plays that are in some sense traditional, that is that put forward readings illustrating Shakespeare's universal genius and that help audiences to understand and appreciate it. It is not unusual, during intervals and after shows, to hear audience members complain that the actors were not in Elizabethan dress or to hear those well-versed in the play grumble about changes made to the script. The architecture of the Royal Shakespeare Theatre reinforces these expectations with its proscenium-arch stage that has resisted all attempts at modification and has been criticized by generations of directors and reviewers for its inflexibility. Robert Shaughnessy argues that the theatre's "predominantly pictorial mode of Shakespearean production," where viewers sit in a darkened auditorium separated from a remote spectacle they can only passively observe, sets up a consumerist relationship between spectators and stage (Shaughnessy 1994: 19). As he points out, the seat prices replicate this dynamic as well, with spectators paying increasingly higher prices for the closer and more central seats (Shaughnessy 1994: 20). By presenting Shakespeare in a space that remains inaccessible to viewers, RSC productions on the main stage work against political engagement with the play. Shakespeare becomes a product that viewers can buy, a commodity whose presence is confirmed not just by the ticket prices but by the souvenir shops and the larger-than-life photos from past productions hanging in the lobbies and corridors. For those visitors to Stratford who have spent the day doing the Shakespeare sights – his birthplace, his house, his daughter's house, his grave – going to the RSC is one last step on the Shakespeare tour.[8]

In such a context, the tension between patriarchal script and feminist intervention can also be seen as a tension between Shakespeare as commercial package and as object of inquiry. While a feminist director may see him as a playwright whose politics should be interrogated, his or her Stratford audience is more likely to see him as a playwright to be consumed. Michael Bogdanov's 1978 RSC production of *The Taming of the Shrew* famously exploited this tension by welcoming his audience with an Italianate set that fitted smoothly into proscenium-arch, pictorial expectations. This set – and its accompanying traditional projection of Shakespeare – was then demolished during what appeared to be a fight between a drunken male audience member and a female usher. This couple turned out to be an updated Sly and Hostess, who then became Petruchio and Katherine. By literally destroying the timeless Bard and replacing him with a twentieth-century version, Bogdanov strove to jolt the audience into seeing the piece through new eyes, eyes that would be willing to see it as an indictment of male violence against women rather than as a comedy. Some in the audience were shocked into a re-evaluation of Shakespeare's play. Michael Billington, reviewer for the *Guardian*, wondered "whether there is any reason to revive a play that seems totally offensive to our age and our society"; his conclusion was that "it should be put back firmly and squarely on the shelf" (Billington 1993: 124). Others, however, responded to this production as evidence of the play's farcical possibilities, continuing to value it as comedy.[9]

The tensions between traditional comedy, feminist inquiry and audience expectations were even more strongly present for Gale Edwards. In an interview with Elizabeth Schafer after the production had closed, she is caustic about the challenges the play presents a female director:

> A woman directing *The Taming of the Shrew*, whoever she is, might as well get a loaded shotgun and put it against her temple, because half the critics will be disappointed and will criticise it if the view of the play is not radical and feminist because they expect that from a woman; then the other half will shoot you down in flames because you're doing a feminist, "limited" view of a play which is meant to be about the surrender of love. So you *cannot* possibly win. You're absolutely fucked.
>
> (Schafer 1998: 57; emphasis in original)

Unlike Bogdanov, who was convinced that his interpretation was true to Shakespeare's intentions, Edwards could not pretend that she was going to be faithful to the play: "My theory about *The Taming of the Shrew* is that it is about the surrender of love and it *is* about her giving up everything and saying, 'I love you and you can tread on my hand.' That is the right way to do it and I couldn't do that production. That was a *huge* artistic and moral dilemma for me" (Schafer 1998: 71; emphasis in original). Edwards only agreed to direct *Shrew* because the temptation to work at the RSC was so strong (see Alderson 1995, Cornwell 1995, Schafer 1998: 71). However, having taken on the play, she found herself confronted not only by her own hesitations but by the demands of others:

> There is a tremendous pressure when a woman takes on a text like this, that somehow this woman is going to solve the play, a play we've been wrestling with for years, or enlighten us or turn it on its head. . . . People don't think, gee, a man is going to direct *King Lear*, this'll be really good because a man is directing. If I directed *Hamlet*, as I have directed *King Lear*, *The Winter's Tale* and *The Tempest*, I would not be subject to this amount of scrutiny or interest. And therein lies the rub. It's what part of the play is about isn't it? . . . How strange it is to be a strong woman.
>
> (Alderson 1995)

Acutely aware of the contradictions inherent in being a woman directing a play about taming women and of the vulnerability involved with doing so at a prominent national theatre, Edwards could have been frozen by the responsibilities placed on her. Instead, the similarities she saw between her situation and Katherine's became a way of revealing those demands and throwing them back to her audience.

Gale Edwards' *Shrew*

Caught between viewers' contradictory desires for a traditional comedy and a feminist indictment, Edwards chose to offer both: the scripted narrative of a happy love story between a shrew and the man who tames her was played out on stage alongside a critique of that narrative. By alternating between these two stories, Edwards made visible the gaps and silences of Shakespeare's script and put the burden of "solving" the play onto her audience. Instead of creating a story for Katherine that provided a rationale for her behavior and thoughts, this production emphasized its absence. Katherine's silence was neither self-explanatory nor readily subsumed into a happy ending, but rather it was something that audiences were forced to confront.

Edwards' production of *Shrew* made it clear that the frame and the taming story were centered on and driven by their male heroes. The performance opened with Sly tossed out into a storm by his wife (Edwards' substitution for the Hostess) and falling asleep into a compensatory dream starring himself as Petruchio and his wife as Katherine. By setting up the taming as a male fantasy, Edwards allowed the script to play out its patriarchal storyline and made questions about what Katherine is feeling irrelevant: she behaves as she does because that is what Sly/Petruchio wishes. But by casting Josie Lawrence as Katherine, Edwards disrupted Petruchio's control. Lawrence is a well-known comic with her own television series (*Josie*) and a regular on the popular improvisational sketch show *Whose Line is it Anyway?* and her fame generated power on stage. While Shakespeare's script suggests that Petruchio controls the story – his words dominate the play – Edwards' production prioritized verbal and physical comedy. The affections of the audience gravitated towards the person who made them laugh, creating a rapport that shaped how they reacted to events on stage. Lawrence's comic persona established Katherine as an appealing character from her first entrance, snarling at her sister's suitors. She walked on stage as if she owned it, setting the tone in the early scenes by taking control of Katherine's image. Her belittlement of the suitors ridiculed their depiction of her as a shrew. They appeared weak and foolish, while she seemed strong and smart, not so much shrewish as impatient with their ineptitude. Her first scene with Petruchio began with him quaking before her, nervously calling her "Kate" as his desire to establish his mastery floundered in the face of her presence. But Edwards refused to allow the production to settle into a story of Katherine's strength. While Lawrence/Katherine began the wooing scene in a position of power, Siberry/Petruchio was soon is successful in controlling the laughter – a pattern of competition for control over each other and the audience that continued throughout the production. Using Lawrence's appeal to counter that of Petruchio, Edwards allowed the audience to fluctuate between finding the taming plot compelling and revolting.

The most graphic examples of these alternating stories came with the contrast between the scenes set in Petruchio's house and the later reconciliation as the couples were on their way to Bianca's wedding. These two depictions of their relationship stood in stark contrast and neither one could erase the presence of the other. During their stay at his house, Katherine and Petruchio's marriage was represented as consisting of his violent domination of her. Although the initial banquet scene was played for laughs, with the servants and Petruchio juggling the food across the room, it was also implicitly violent: Petruchio pretended to beat his servants and Katherine hid under the table from the flying meats. By the time the stage had cleared and Petruchio re-emerged to deliver his soliloquy, "Thus have I politicly begun my reign" (4.1.169–92), the tone was deadly serious. During the soliloquy, which Siberry delivered to the audience, Katherine emerged upstage accompanied by solemn music. She looked just as Petruchio described her, starved and exhausted, and her onstage presence graphically illustrated the physical actions behind his falconry metaphors. She literally upstaged Siberry/Petruchio, a material presence that his voice could not erase and an extratextual reminder of the violence of Shakespeare's script. Katherine remained on stage during the next scene, the walls of the set moving to box her in on three sides; her trapped misery counteracted the wooing games Bianca was playing with Tranio, Lucentio and Hortensio, and reminded us precisely of what is taught at the taming school Hortensio said he would attend. After their exit, Lawrence addressed the audience with her opening lines of the next scene: "The more my wrong, the more his spite appears. / What, did he marry me to famish me?" (4.3.2–14) By making Katherine's first thirteen lines a soliloquy instead of a speech to Grumio, Edwards gave Lawrence/Katherine equal dramatic time with Siberry/Petruchio, counteracting his description of the taming with her experience of it. What the audience saw and heard invited them to judge Petruchio's treatment of Katherine as cruel, and to sympathize with her confusion and despair.

But when Petruchio and Katherine were on their way to Bianca's wedding and he asked her to agree with him that the sun is the moon, their relationship was presented as one of mutual appreciation and loving flirtation. Katherine, although a bit slow to pick up her cues at first, soon responded to Petruchio's name games, assuring him flirtatiously that "sun it is not, when you say it is not, / And the moon changes even as your mind" (4.6.20–1). Twisting her finger at the side of his head to indicate that he is crazy, she was about to kiss him when they were interrupted by the appearance of Vincentio. Katherine's encounter with Vincentio provided an opportunity to continue her sexual flirting with Petruchio. Taking his suggestion to embrace the "fair lovely maid" (4.5.34) one step further, she looked at Petruchio so that he could acknowledge and appreciate her challenge in wondering aloud at the lucky maid's future bedfellow. When Petruchio corrected her by pointing out that Vincentio is an old man, Katherine graciously acknowledged her mistake. There was no trace of the earlier cruelty and power imbalance in their marriage. Instead, they were presented as willing participants in a comic love story.

The deferred kiss returned as a climax in the next scene. Having just witnessed the discovery of Lucentio's real identity and his marriage to Bianca, Katherine suggested to her husband that they follow the group home. He refused to do so until she gave him a kiss, which, she made clear, she was reluctant to do "in the midst of the street" (5.1.125). Petruchio insisted, and she complied; the couple then shared what Siberry has described as "a big, long 'screen' kiss" (Siberry 1998: 56). Edwards' production set up this moment as a willing reconciliation between the two, who then walked off arm in arm, accompanied by a glowing sunset and swelling music. The kiss in the street came as a seemingly natural conclusion to Katherine and Petruchio's growing flirtation in the earlier sun/moon scene, and the audience on the first night I saw the play applauded the moment loudly. Although the movie stereotypes of pink sunsets and passionate clinches also send up the moment, the embrace in the street fulfilled the earlier promise of a kiss, and the audience responded with relief.[10]

Despite their wildly differing natures, no effort was made to provide a coherent transition from the depiction of Petruchio's cruelty and Katherine's despair to that of the loving couple we saw a few scenes later. No explanation was given for Katherine's acquiescing to Petruchio's sun/moon games, let alone why she seemed to be charmed by him. Nor does the happy kiss erase the violent taming: Katherine entered the street scene eating what appeared to be a chicken leg, a visual and unmistakable reminder of her earlier starving self. Despite that reminder, and the obvious implication that she was only allowed to eat as a reward for her good behavior in the sun/moon scene, the audience I first saw the play with chose at this moment to endorse the love story over the taming critique. By forcing the audience to recognize the violence of the taming, and then encouraging them to approve the love story, Edwards moved the audience back and forth between the two positions of critiquing and endorsing the patriarchal politics of the playscript without appearing to privilege either. Although the audience's initial attraction to Katherine upset the traditional stereotype of a shrew, their subsequent laughter in the "wooing" scene with Petruchio returned to a masculinist understanding of the plot. The pair of taming soliloquies in the middle of the play undercut the patriarchal plot, but the flirtatious sun/moon debate made that plot seem a pleasant one. The triumphant kiss in the street clinched the love story, only to have that story seem increasingly unlikely as the production moved towards its final moments. It is in these last scenes that Edwards' strategy paid off.

Katherine's final speech, notorious for its extreme submission, carries so much extratextual weight as to be almost unreadable, particularly for those who wish to believe in a universal Shakespeare. The literal text is, perhaps, all too readable – a rhythmically even and generally straightforward lesson on the duties a wife owes her husband. But, if anything, its blatant servility increases the desire to make the speech say something else. For many modern readers and viewers of *The Taming of the Shrew*, this is where the playscript collapses in on itself, the moment where Petruchio's patriarchal domination of Katherine becomes so bitter that the comedy can no longer be sustained. In an oft-cited criticism, George Bernard Shaw wrote in 1897 that

> No man with any decency of feeling can sit it out in the company of a woman without being extremely ashamed of the lord-of-creation moral implied in the wager and the speech put into the woman's own mouth.
>
> (Wilson 1961: 188)

The fact that scholars and reviewers nearly a century later continue to quote Shaw without referring to the context of his article (a dismissal of Garrick's *Catherine and Petruchio* in which he praises Shakespeare's realism) reveals the degree to which the play's ending has become the focal-point of any production or interpretation.[11] As we have seen, directors have frequently adapted the speech to make it more palatable, and feminist scholars repeatedly turn to it as the focus of their inquiries. With all this attention on her words circulating through the cultural energy of the play, Katherine's submission speech bears the burden not only of resolving the playscript and its performance, but of answering the larger issues of gender relationships that reverberate in early twentieth-first-century western culture.

This extratextual burden carried by Katherine's speech became part of the dynamic of Edwards' *Shrew*, which relied on audience expectations to fill in the script's character gaps. When Petruchio and Katherine first entered the scene, she was dressed in a modified version of the dress she and Petruchio had argued about with the tailor. They appeared to be a happily married couple on equal footing with each other. But when Katherine re-entered at Petruchio's bidding, and discovered that he had been betting on her obedience, the entire context and tone of the scene changed. No longer part of a power-sharing couple, Katherine performed her speech of submission but abandoned her husband immediately after. After her disappearance into the toy theatre that appeared upstage (following the exit of the rest of the characters), the play returned to the Sly frame. The broken-hearted Petruchio became newly repentant Sly, who begged his wife's forgiveness when she came to bring him out of the storm. What appeared to be a patriarchal revenge fantasy turned out to be something so horrible that even the plot's creator shunned it. As the summary in the program describes it, "Petruchio slowly realizes what he has been attempting to do to Katherina in the name of love. By the end of the speech his dream has become his nightmare . . ." (Royal Shakespeare Company 1995).

Because the production had vacillated so wildly between contesting and upholding the playscript's patriarchal comedy, viewers found themselves entering Katherine's speech without a solid basis from which to interpret it – would it continue in the vein of a love story or return to a critique of that plot? Rather than appearing clearly as a sincere endorsement or an ironic rejection of the text's message of submission, Lawrence/Katherine's performance of the speech was a blank space waiting to be filled with meaning. Our awareness as viewers of the performative aspects of the moment – our sense that Lawrence/Katherine was reciting a speech rather than releasing thoughts and emotions into words – did not answer the question of what Katherine meant her words to be. Instead of being able to read the moment as a revelation of her character, we were put in the position of reading it as a revelation of our own desires. If this speech was a performance, what was it a performance of? What did we want Katherine to be saying? Typically, actor training and audience

Plate 2 A repentant Petruchio (Michael Siberry) kneeling in front of Katherine (Josie Lawrence) in Gale Edwards' 1995 RSC *Taming of the Shrew*. Reproduced with permission of the Shakespeare Centre Library, Stratford-upon-Avon.

experience set up a psychologically coherent character that develops through the actor's physical embodiment of the textual role. But Edwards and Lawrence radically destabilized that coherency by altering the audience's relationship to the performance. By moving the audience back and forth between incompatible endorsements and critiques of the taming plot, the production replicates in its viewers Katherine's own position within the script, moving from one set-piece to the next with little sense of continuity or development on which to build a unified character. It was impossible for viewers to read the ending as telling Katherine's story, since there was never a clear sense of what "her" story is. All the audience had to go on was its own sense of what was an appropriate ending for the play.

Edwards' production refused to allow its viewers the false luxury of sitting back and having Shakespeare solved for them. This *Shrew* created gaps in the logic of the story that had to be filled by its viewers. In the final moments of the play, the two storylines – taming romance and feminist critique – collided and the audience realized that they could not have it both ways. When Petruchio/Sly (who wanted a happy ending as much as any viewer) realized the mistake of his revenge fantasy,

Edwards created a space for the audience to share his remorse. We realized that our desire for a happy ending implicated us in a regressive and harmful ideology, and thus we recognized the danger of consuming Shakespeare blindly. In this way, Edwards' *Shrew* offered a feminist production that could be presented on the RSC main stage without succumbing to a passive acceptance of its politics.

Whose words are these anyway? The discourses of reviewing

But Edwards' production was not as straightforward as that. The "us" that I have written of, the notion of "our sense as viewers," is a false projection of unity. My description of Edwards' production of *The Taming of the Shrew*, of what it was about, is not one echoed in the production's reviews. Where I saw a production that challenged our assumptions and desires, critics writing for the national press saw only one that failed to meet their traditional interpretations of the play. Throughout their reviews, the same discourses circulated, particularly an emphasis on fidelity to Shakespeare (whether that be textual or thematic) and an insistence on realism. Their notions of what the play meant and which behaviors were realistic joined to create a masculinist vision of *Shrew* that could not allow for Edwards' feminist challenges.

One of the most vehement objections that emerged was to the production's supposed erasure of Shakespeare's text. Protesting that Edwards' minor alterations (substituting Sly's wife for the Hostess, cutting the play's lines after the end of Katherine's submission speech and having Sly reappear remorsefully at the end) meant that her production was not actually of Shakespeare's play, reviewers mixed their own anxieties about gender roles with their beliefs about how Shakespeare should be staged. Benedict Nightingale and John Peter were the most concerned with what they saw as Edwards' violations to the text; in each of their reviews, this complaint was a smokescreen for their fear that she had feminized the Bard. Nightingale, writing for *The Times*, criticized the "cuts and additions that don't even have the excuse of coming from the anonymous ur-play, *The Taming of a Shrew*" and insisted that Sly/Petruchio's remorse at the end of the play was blatantly false to Shakespeare: "What tripe! That may be how the Bard's *Guardian*-reading descendant, Dennis Shakespeare, would have ended the play. Will himself was more robust" (Nightingale 1995).[12]

In the *Sunday Times*, Peter was just as concerned about the play's faithlessness to Shakespeare: "The question is, how many liberties can you take with a play in order to interpret it? What is the difference between interpreting a play and making it say what *you* want it to say? Do dead playwrights have rights?" (Peter 1995; emphasis in original). Although Nightingale and Peter used textual changes as the ostensible bases for their objections, their real charge was that Edwards had betrayed Shakespeare's gender politics. Nightingale thought that the ending was too soft, playing on right-wing suspicions about the masculinity of left-wing men: the remorse over a patriarchal taming was something that would appeal to the sensitive men of the *Guardian* crowd (the newspaper furthest on the left of the broadsheets' political spectrum) but not to the readers of the *Times* (on the right), who are the inheritors of Shakespeare's robustness. Similarly, Peter's feeling that the framework set the play up as "a piece of theatrical marriage counseling" which has the fault of "turning Shakespeare into a tedious busybody who thinks of the theatre as a moral fitness centre where suitable exercises will tone you up for lifelong maturity" invoked suspicions about weak men whose wives drag them to counselors (Peter 1995). For both reviewers, Shakespeare is more macho ("robust" and not a "busybody" who needs to work out in a fitness center) than the vision Edwards invokes.

While Nightingale and Peter thought that Edwards should have been true to Shakespeare's male spirit, they also acknowledged *Shrew*'s problematic sexual politics, setting up a conundrum that makes it nearly impossible for a feminist director to stage the play. Commenting on the frequent appearance of *Shrew* at the RSC, Nightingale said that "It would be nice to believe that this is because the company is conscientiously exploring the complexities of a politically incorrect text; but the reason is surely that it is a comic crowd-pleaser with a mildly naughty reputation." However, Edwards' production, he claimed, "fails the play for it is neither very funny nor makes much sense of its sexual politics" (Nightingale 1995). Since Nightingale also insisted that the play's male hero should not feel remorse, it seems that making sense of *Shrew*'s sexual politics allows only for the portrayal of relentless sexism.

For Peter as well, the sexual politics need to be made sense of, but the ending of this production failed because it preaches: "This is not a Shakespearian [*sic*] ending at all, not because Shakespeare is a male chauvinist or a cheery optimist but because this ending is like a sermon" (Peter 1995). But being like a sermon is hardly a flaw – a sermon is exactly what Katherine's last speech was intended to be, designated in the playscript as her lesson to Bianca and the Widow on how to be a good wife and modeled after pre-Reformation wedding sermons. Peter's complaint seems not to be that it preaches, but that in this production it preached something inappropriate. His own belief is that the play's answers about gender politics are "evasive," but he also feels that "Shakespeare is more on [Petruchio's] side than on [Katherine's]" (Peter 1995). Peter leaves as little room to maneuver as Nightingale: both imply that the way to make sense of Shakespeare's gender politics is to accommodate rather than challenge them. Feminist directors and actors are thus both eliminated from any possible "Shakespearean" production of *Shrew*.

Although other reviewers were concerned less with textual fidelity and more with distancing themselves from the play's misogyny, they too relied on narrow definitions of what *Shrew* could be about. Michael Billington in the *Guardian*, Michael Coveney in the *Observer*, Nicholas de Jongh in the *Evening Standard*, Louise Doughty in the *Mail on Sunday*, John Gross in the *Sunday Telegraph*, Jack Tinker in the *Daily Mail* and Irving Wardle in the *Independent on Sunday* all pointed out the ways in which *The Taming of the Shrew* is unpalatable for a modern audience. For the most part, these critics focused on Katherine's final submission speech, describing it as making "the least pro-feminist among us curl their toes" (Tinker 1995). Although a few of the reviewers mentioned "the repugnant central theme" (Gross 1995) of "Shakespeare's breath-takingly misogynistic tale" (Doughty 1995) and "the bullying of Katherina, the shrew, into submission by a wooing policy of starvation, humiliation and psychological warfare" (Coveney 1995), the play's unpleasantness is seen as resting almost entirely in its final moments. This focus on the play's ending denies the broader ways in which *Shrew*'s misogyny is incorporated into its script and in this case it clearly limited reviewers' ability to recognize Edwards' interventions. There is a sense in many of the reviews of their paying lipservice in acknowledging *Shrew*'s troublesome politics; once it is out of the way, reviewers are free to participate in the play's structural misogyny.

Reactions to the depiction of the central characters in Edwards' production showed how many reviewers' expectations were shaped by masculinist assumptions. A recurring complaint was that Josie Lawrence's Katherine was not shrewish enough. Wrote John Gross, "It is as though either [Lawrence] or Edwards or both of them found it hard to admit that there could really be such a thing as a shrew" (Gross 1995), and John Peter complained, "Her nastiness in the early scenes is unconvincing, rather as if she were doing it under duress" (Peter 1995). Their longing for a vicious shrew reveals an important structural feature of the playscript and of Edwards' production. *The Taming of the Shrew* functions as a comedy when viewers think that such a taming is inherently funny – that there are women who deserve to be taught a lesson in how to behave.[13] In the *Financial Times*, Alastair Macaulay explained that it is a mistake to be offended by the play's depiction of gender relationships since "The comedy is that Katherine is a *shrew*"; he later criticized the production for being "too timid" to make her so (Macaulay 1995). As these reviewers noted, Lawrence's Katherine was not typically shrewish, rather she was a funny and self-possessed woman, a characterization that makes us question the nature of shrewishness. With their insistence that such women do exist, however, reviewers missed the production's questioning of the fantasies men project onto women (Bianca was as much a manipulator of the role constructed for her as Katherine) and ignored Edwards' deliberate alterations to the traditional play.

Complaints that Katherine was not shrewish enough were matched by those that Petruchio and Sly were not manly enough. The characters' final moments of repentance were stunningly unrealistic for some reviewers. "What macho fantasy includes remorse?" asked Irving Wardle (1995), and John Gross complained, "It isn't enough for him to be shamed when he wakes from his dream: impatient feminism demands that he has to be shamed within the dream as well" (Gross 1995). By refusing to admit the possibility of Sly's remorse, however, they refused to consider Edwards' suggestion that men might not want subservient wives. This insistence on strict gendered categories – shrews are shrewish and men are macho – suggests that these objections to Edwards' production are based not on its portrayal of character but on its politics.

Working with contradictory interpretations

Why does my reading of Edwards' *Shrew* differ so fundamentally from those of the reviewers? The answer lies partly in our belonging to separate interpretive communities, to use Stanley Fish's phrase (Fish 1980). Certainly the Shakespeare scholar and the newspaper reviewer require different interpretive criteria to make sense of what is on stage. However, if a simple division of scholar versus reviewer might make sense in theory, in practice there are too many individual differences to be explained: not all academics and not all reviewers reacted the same way to Edwards' *Shrew*.[14] While the notion of interpretive communities is helpful for revealing the different criteria readers are schooled in, it also obscures the ideological factors complicating the process of interpretation by relying on an abstract sense of "the reader." As Janet Staiger points out, readers are neither homogenous nor coherent: "each spectator is a complex and contradictory construction of such self-identities as gender, sexual preference, class, race, and ethnicity. The pertinence of each self-identity might at times dominate the others, perhaps overdetermine or contradict as well" (Staiger 1992: 13). Because "the interpretive event occurs at the intersection of multiple determinations" (Staiger 1992: 48) the resulting interpretation is not coherent.

An incoherent interpretation can also be the result of diachronic differences in self-identity – we may not be the same person while watching a play as we are later, when we write about it. My own viewing history of Edwards' *Shrew* illustrates the dramatic changes that can occur in the process of interpretation. When I first saw Edwards' production, I did not think it a successful feminist staging of the play. I was left feeling dissatisfied, unable to make sense of what I had just seen: a production that was unable to control its audience, unable to prevent viewers from applauding a kiss between an abusive husband and his starving wife, unable to make up its mind about who Katherine was and how we were supposed to feel about her. I was haunted by the scene with the tailor, which seemed to undercut the sympathy created for the starving Katherine by showing her to be as concerned about shopping and nice clothes as she was about survival and autonomy. And I was particularly bothered by her final speech, which seemed to be poorly delivered since I could find no way of understanding it either as sincere or ironic. At the time, I was in the midst of researching the RSC Women's Group and I wanted Edwards' *Shrew* to be its opposite, a clear-cut indictment of masculinist Shakespeare. It was only after a few months that I began to reconsider my initial disappointment. Once I started to think about the problems of discontinuous subjectivity and how that could be represented on stage, I began to find a way of viewing Edwards' production that made more sense of it. And once I began to think about feminist Shakespeare's relationship to the proscenium arch of the RSC main stage, the production made even more sense to me. After a year of hard thinking about this *Shrew*, it began to coalesce.

My initial reaction to the production has, until now, remained hidden. The coherent analysis I gave earlier, with its praise for Edwards' sophisticated exposé of gender relations, overwrote my earlier confusion. I am not alone in this rewriting. Peter Holland similarly claims of the production, "it was only in retrospect that I felt any confidence in having followed the meaning that was unfolding. . . . my high opinion of its intellectual rigour only came *after* the event, overcoming my doubts" (Holland 1997: 240; emphasis in original). One way in which to understand this change of opinion is to see it as evidence of growth: given enough time, Holland and I were able to "solve" Edwards' production. But such an understanding is misleading. Despite the chronological sequence, my different interpretations are not teleological. The final, positive assessment of *Shrew* came not from a return to the production itself, but from a return to my memories of it. Indeed, if it is a "solution" at all, it is more of a solution to my initial reaction than to the production. It might explain Edwards' *Shrew* in a more positive light, but it also explains my reaction more favorably: my distraught response to the first viewing becomes an illustration of the emotions Edwards was striving to provoke. In other words, the *Shrew* I saw was the *Shrew* I wanted to see, both as I watched it and during my subsequent analysis.

Although the interpretation that I presented as a description of Edwards' *Shrew* is also a description of my memory and a recuperation of my experience, it is still useful as a tool for examining the production. By comparing the wide range of contradictory reactions, we can discover the most compelling aspects not just of this production but of Shakespeare in performance more generally. The question of coherent character crops up repeatedly throughout the many *Shrew*s that I have traced in this chapter. My own analysis depends on a tension between incompatible Katherines and on the audience's longing to reconcile the script's gaps into a unified character. The reviewers repeatedly insisted that neither Petruchio nor Katherine adhered to the coherent, realistic depictions of machismo and shrewishness they read into Shakespeare's script. Even Edwards' characterization of her relationship to *Shrew* is marked by a struggle for consistency: torn between her beliefs that the playscript is about a woman's surrender to her husband and her own inability to endorse such a story, Edwards places herself as an incoherent storyteller, one who occupies two subjectivities simultaneously.

These views of Edwards' *Shrew* emphasize the play's contradictions and the ways these lead to a discontinuous Katherine. But Penny Gay's reading of the production turns on precisely the opposite point. For Gay, the strength of Edwards' *Shrew* was its "psychologically convincing and realistic portrayal of the story of one woman married to a boor" (Gay 1999: 45). Where I saw a series of set-pieces and no through-line, Gay located a very specific turning-point for Katherine, one that made her into a completely coherent character. Earlier in this chapter, I insisted that no effort was made to show the transition from the downtrodden Katherine at Petruchio's house to the loving and playful Katherine in the sun/moon scene; this discontinuity was an important part of my analysis of how Edwards' production worked. Gay, however, points out exactly where the moment of transition occurred:

> At the end of this scene [4.3] she [Katherine] was left alone and she gave a determined nod, as if to say "I know what must be done" – as we saw in the "sun and moon" scene, where with somewhat amused exasperation she humored Petruchio.
>
> (Gay 1999: 45)

This nod is an important moment in Gay's analysis, so central that she is at pains to legitimize her reading of it through a footnote: "Josie Lawrence confirmed my reading of this gesture in conversation on September 28, 1995" (Gay 1999: 50).[15] This "determined nod," however, was not as noticeable or transparent as Gay suggests. Neither I nor Barbara Hodgdon caught it – I never noticed it, and I saw the production twice, and Hodgdon saw the production three times and, in an email to me, confirmed that she noticed no such nod.

I am not denying that this nod was something Lawrence intended to signify as a turning-point, nor am I asserting that Gay is mistaken in describing its effect in creating a continuous character. I am suggesting that viewers will often see what they need to see in order to make sense of a performance. For example, Ralph Berry describes a *Twelfth Night* in which a teddy-bear slipped from Malvolio's robes; although his companion and the reviews in the papers also saw a teddy-bear, a conversation with the actor revealed it to have been a doll (Berry 1985: 596). Seeing a teddy-bear instead of a doll is a relatively minor discrepancy. This kind of slip might easily make emotional sense to the viewer: for a viewer fond of teddy-bears, for example, it could add a degree of vulnerability to Malvolio's character. Similarly, Gay's discovery of Lawrence's nod makes emotional sense within the context of her search for a psychologically real character. For Gay, the success of Edwards' production lay in its realistic depiction of Katherine. Her proof lies not just in her discovery of the nod or her reaction to Lawrence's performance, but in the reaction of her fellow audience members:

> My own random surveys of members of the audience reveal that the production had many women very excited by its combination of bold theatricality and a powerfully realistic reading of the central part. Most men were more ambivalent, when not downright

condemnatory, but their critiques were carefully aimed not at the reading of Katherine and Petruchio's relationship, but at the "stylistic incoherence" of the production.

(Gay 1999: 46)

In Gay's reading, the women were able to recognize the "real" story of the play by endorsing its "powerfully realistic reading" whereas the men could only see "stylistic incoherence." Realism is her highest praise, in terms of both the production's artistic goals and its feminist ones.

Just as Gay's reading of the production turns on the connection between realism and feminism, so does Barbara Hodgdon's, only by inverting the location for praise. Hodgdon is specifically interested in Edwards' production as an illustration of how women can disrupt the Shakespearean narrative by creating "a new characterology" through their performances (Hodgdon 1998: 38). Hodgdon focuses her attention on how the sight of Lawrence's body provides an alternative to the farcical script that empowers Petruchio, replacing Katherine's scripted silence with Lawrence's performance as a subjected body: "Proposing sight as a means of making Kate's silence readable as a counter-narrative, Edwards' staging calls attention to the bridling of a script that, by calling attention to the bridling of her voice, constructs Kate as a partial subject" (1998: 31). This manner of reading allows Hodgdon to understand the scene with the tailor as a moment that actively fractures the male text:

> Petruchio has ripped both sleeves and the bodice from the tailor's new gown, producing two images of stripped women: Kate in an underdress, the dressmaker's dummy nude to the waist. Watching the scene unfold across an image of her own dismembered body, Kate's is an interrupting "third eye". . . . For as the men (at stage right) banter over "tak[ing] up my mistress' gown to his master's use," Kate crosses to the dummy (downstage left) and sinks down beside it, caressing the discarded pieces. Fracturing the stage space, her gest decisively marks off the men's locker-room jokes from a feminine narrative of loss and desire that rivets the gaze.

(Hodgdon 1998: 31)

In contrast to Gay's reading of the scene, this is not about a transition in Katherine's character. Hodgdon's reading of the moment is a deeply theorized reflection on the nature of subjectivity and the complicity of gender and gaze. In Hodgson's feminist story, a unified

Katherine is not needed, neither emotionally nor to provide a sense of narrative logic.

The consistent focal-point of character formation suggests, not only that the problems written into Katherine and *Shrew* are difficult to resolve, but that the question of what constitutes a character is a pressing one in performed Shakespeare. The problem of Katherine that the various viewers raised (how do we make sense of who she is?) is also a problem of reading (how do we make sense of the text?) and a problem of reception (how do we know what the text is?). The different viewers of Edwards' *Shrew* saw different Katherines and different *Shrew*s, some of which strove towards a coherent self while others reveled in the disintegration of character. The repeated insistence on character coherency as either the source of a successful production or the very factor that needs to be interrogated in order to create a successful production suggests that this is an issue not only pertinent to Edwards' *Shrew*, but fundamental to all performed Shakespeare.

Epilogue
The language of theatre

The RSC generally strives for a transparent theatrical language – a style of performance that lets its audience concentrate on *what* is being presented rather than *how* it is presented. This illusion of transparency allows the company and its audience to imagine that they are able to access Shakespeare's real meanings through a play's performance. However, other producers of the plays make the encounter between playscript and theatrical language more visible. Such defamiliarization of performance methods makes it impossible to imagine that we can discover the true Shakespeare on stage.

The University of Pennsylvania's Theatre Arts production of *Two Gentlemen of Verona*, directed by Cary Mazer in February 1999, was an example of performed Shakespeare that took the language of theatre as seriously as it did the language of the playscript. Mazer's *Two Gentlemen* was a story within a story, one enacted by an all-female cast that neither transformed male characters into female ones nor performed in male drag. The continual disjuncture between gender and actor and character highlighted the creative process of performance and negated the desire to see the women's performance as a neutral realization of Shakespeare's meaning. The production's frame story was told by female actors playing female characters and two male actors playing male characters. As the audience filled their seats, they found a stage covered with gym equipment, including treadmills, stairmasters, free weights and a bench press; women, wearing gym clothes, entered the stage and began to exercise on the various machines. Even after the audience had filled the theatre, the women continued working out. It appeared that this scene could continue indefinitely, and it was only the men's entrance that altered its dynamics. Walking noisily in, the two men kicked one of the women off the bench press and proceeded to take over the machine. Loudly and ostentatiously encouraging each other with fairly light weights – "push it, push it!" "come on, one more!" – the men finished their set after a few minutes and departed with a "thanks ladies." After their exit, the women, starting with the one who had been kicked off the weight machine, began to parody the men's macho performance. Out of this parody emerged the performance of *Two Gentlemen*: the woman who had been kicked off the machine took on the role of Valentine, her friend played Proteus, and soon everyone in the room had joined in.

It was never made clear how these women happened to perform *Two Gentlemen* (Had they previously memorized Shakespeare's script and chosen at this moment to perform it? Did they start telling a story that happened to be in iambic pentameter?), but the question of the literal relationship between their performance and Shakespeare's script was not the primary focus. Instead, the impact on the actors of doing this script emerged as the main story. This telling of *Two Gentlemen* started off as a story about male bonding and male posturing, a performance that mocked macho notions of masculinity. As the women's telling of the story progressed, however, their attitude shifted. By the time we came to Proteus' attempted rape of Silvia, the tone was no longer one of mockery but of discomfort. The performance began by making fun of Valentine and Proteus, but it ended in horror at Silvia's suffering – suffering in which not only Valentine and Proteus were agents but in which the women playing those roles were complicit. After the attempted rape and attempted reconciliation, the frame characters stumbled through the rest of Shakespeare's script and exited the gym as quickly as possible.[1]

As a brief description of how this production dealt with Shakespeare's script, this account omits the most important aspects of the performance. For while Shakespeare's text informed some of the production's choices, this *Two Gentlemen* was equally shaped by its rehearsal process and acting language. Mazer chose *Two Gentlemen* because he was looking for a play that could offer roles to four of his acting students, women who were doing their senior thesis project.[2] He had long thought that the only way to handle the play was to use an all-female cast that might distance the production from the script's troubling

Plate 3 Proteus (left, Julie Fitzpatrick) comforts Valentine (Vanessa Mizzone) as he prepares to depart for the forest in Cary Mazer's 1999 Theatre arts production of *Two Gentlemen of Verona* at the University of Pennsylvania. Reproduced by permission of Cary Mazer. More images from this production are available online at http://dept.english.upenn.edu/~tharts/two_gents.html

gender politics; here was the perfect opportunity to engage with the play in this way. Mazer was also interested in a physical approach to acting, drawing on Sanford Meisner and building on his own sense of the problems inherent in using modern, Stanislavsky-based acting to explore early modern characters. This production of *Two Gentlemen* was as much about, as Mazer phrases it, "experimenting with grounding things in physical tasks" as it was about interpreting Shakespeare's script.[3] His interest in physical tasks and the need for a setting that could work as a female community led Mazer to set the production in a gym.

During the rehearsal process, the group made an important discovery about using the physical objects found in the gym as substitutes for actions represented in the playscript. The actors had been working with exercises on transforming objects drawn from Joseph Chaiken and the Open Theatre. Mazer describes the process:

> You throw a physical object into the center of a circle. One of the actors gets up, picks it up, and uses it as something for which it was not intended. Someone else comes in and joins the person using that object in the way [she] has just invented to use it, or jumps in, picks up the object and uses it as something else, and then the person who is already in the scene has to adapt to what the object now is. And then somebody else comes in and before you know it, all eight or nine people are in it and transforming it.

Such transformation exercises are not unusual. But in this rehearsal process, the actors found themselves relying on the objects' intended uses in order to convey other actions. Using a free weight to brush your teeth did not mean using it with the movement of a toothbrush but, as Mazer describes, "using the object as the object was designed to be used." Brushing your teeth was shown by doing curls with the weight rather than moving it up and down against your teeth. Instead of transforming an object, "you're investing in the reality of the object and the physical task of using the object to mean something else." Discovering this non-transformative process led to the theatrical language of the play. Doing bicep curls could represent hugging, and participating in an aerobics class could stand for searching through the forest. Some of the physical objects and actions acquired a systematic set of meanings. Water bottles represented letters, and drinking from the bottle meant reading. Kissing became two characters sharing a water bottle, and the attempted rape was Proteus forcing Silvia to drink from his bottle and then emptying its contents over her. The visual metaphors established with this use of objects both clarified the physical actions on stage and highlighted their thematic links.

The shift from transformation to investment in physical reality also shifted the relationship between the actors and the roles they played. The actors were not transformed into the frame characters, nor were the frame characters transformed into the Shakespearean characters. Instead, the actors, that is, the women behind the women behind the men and women of the inner play, were always present both as themselves and as their characters. Mazer's original interest in using an all-female cast was to separate actor and role:

> The reason for the starting point of all women was to allow for the possibility that we can see some distance between the frame character/actor and the role she is playing, so that by enacting the attempted rape (and not just that) we wouldn't necessarily be endorsing that behavior.

The investment in physical reality, however, led ultimately to a closeness of actor, frame character and Shakespearean role. It was impossible not to be aware of the actors behind the roles when they were clad in gym clothes and engaged in physical exercises; if the free weights used to indicate hugging were always visible as weights, the biceps lifting them remained the actors', and not the characters'. The make-up of the audience – heavily dominated by the actors' families, friends, classmates and teachers – furthered the awareness of the actors' bodies. This heightened physical presence meant that the actors ended up being crucially present in the very actions Mazer originally intended to distance. Proteus attempted to rape Silvia, but the female frame character playing Proteus was complicit in his violence, and the woman playing Silvia was herself the subject of assault.

For the actors behind the frame characters, this dynamic shifted their relationship to both the frame story and the inner play. Tammy Dong, the actor who played Lance, recoiled from the assault scene when it was first rehearsed and, according to Mazer, said she did not want to be in the play. Mazer recalls her coming to him and saying, "my character spends the entire play making these awful sexist jokes about women, that last scene with Speed in particular, and when I see now what men can do to women, I don't feel good anymore about what I did as Lance." Mazer's response was,

> Well, who's the "you" in that sentence? Because the "you" can be who you are and it can be your frame character, and ideally it's both. We've just found your journey in this play. Your journey is from someone who can, for whatever variety of reasons, have fun playing the role of Lance and on seeing this spectacle, realize that it's something you're not happy doing.

Instead of being able to distance themselves from what their characters were doing, the actors and frame characters found themselves suddenly present in the moment and implicated in its events.

The story of this play was not, as it turned out, about Proteus and Valentine's friendship or about women's mockery of male communities. Instead, this was a *Two Gentlemen* that focused on coming to terms with the horrors surrounding us and with our own capacity to be brutal. As Mazer describes,

> It became a story about the ability of these particular women finding themselves in a situation where they are playing men starting from a position of mockery and, because of the actor vocabulary of finding the moment, finding that they could do things as men which they don't like men doing, that horrifies the men when the men discover themselves doing it, and horrifies the women not only because men are doing it, but because they are capable of doing it.

The importance of actor vocabulary, as Mazer notes, was fundamental to the story the production created. Because the actors emphasized the physical grounding of their behavior, their efforts to "find the moment" focused on the immediacy of what was happening. Rather than trying to create a through-line or coherent psychological narrative to explain the desires of a character, the actors strove to embody the dynamics of each scene as it happened. Because the actors concentrated on a physical embodiment rather than a psychological profile, the frame characters found themselves doing things as the Shakespeare characters that they, and the actors playing them, would not have chosen to do. Another way of understanding how their actor vocabulary worked is that it did not require a consistency either within a character's actions or between roles. A different type of reading or rehearsal process might have created explanations for the characters' behavior, rationalizing the brutality of the ending or diminishing it. But the need to be fully present and physically committed to each moment of the play, in combination with the allowance for a separation between frame character and Shakespeare role, created a performance that neither erased nor condoned the horror of what happened.

In this production, the use of a non-Shakespearean performance style highlighted the encounter between script and performance and created meanings on stage that could not have been found in the text alone. Without an appreciation for its theatrical language, we would not recognize the lessons it points up about community, identity and the effect of cultural expectations on our behavior. Shakespeare's script is not irrelevant to the meaning of this production. Without the

Shakespeare play at its core, it would be impossible to understand the patterns of male behavior that drive the production; its gender explorations are made through the cultural authority of the playwright and the generations of transmission of his text. But to see this *Two Gentlemen of Verona* only as an interpretation of the text trivializes its relationship to Shakespeare and fails to acknowledge the work that the production does in creating meanings that address its audiences' lives.

Understanding a performance of a Shakespeare play, then, requires an examination of variables that we do not always or easily consider. We must take into account not just Shakespeare's script (or scripts, in the case of the multi–version plays like *Hamlet* and *King Lear*) but myriad factors that the discipline of English literature has taught us to think of as theatrical ephemera: how actors are trained to read and perform, how a theatre company is organized, what cultural concerns enter the rehearsal room and performance space, who goes to see the performance, where the performance space is and its relationship to the surrounding locale and to its audience. Not only must these elements become part of our analysis of Shakespeare, but our own position in relation to Shakespeare must be examined. After all this work with theatrical ephemera, one is left with an equally ephemeral result: a performance of Shakespeare that reflects the individual viewer's perceptions and desires as much as it does those of Shakespeare or the director. Such attention to the apparently transient conditions that shape performance and the localized meaning of each interpretation of a performance goes against the grain of how most Shakespeare scholars are trained. The permanence and importance of Shakespeare are tossed aside for the fleeting fancies of the stage. But going against the grain is just what we need to do if we want to open up the possibility not just of new Shakespeares but future Shakespeares.

To say that performance is ephemeral implies that text is substantial, permanent and accessible. But such a claim is as false as the belief that performed Shakespeare is shaped only by its relationship to the text and contains only one meaning. As has been repeatedly demonstrated, Shakespeare's text is neither a singular entity nor a readily accessible one. The printed work that we think of as Shakespeare's has passed through hundreds of hands other than his own, including those of Renaissance actors and printers and the long line of editors from Rowe onwards. In the process of printing and editing, much can happen to change what was written. Ferdinand's praise of Prospero in *The Tempest* is one such instance: "Let me live here ever! / So rare a wondered father and a wise / Makes this place paradise" (4.1.122–4). Why, one might ask, is his father-in-law here but not his wife? As Stephen Orgel notes, "Critics since the eighteenth century have expressed a nagging worry about the fact that in celebrating his betrothal, Ferdinand's paradise includes Prospero but not Miranda" (Orgel 1988: 228–9). Shakespeare's earliest editors, Rowe and Malone, changed "wise" to "wife" in their texts on logical grounds, while later nineteenth-century editors included "wife" in their lists of variants; "Nevertheless, after 1895, the wife became invisible: bibliographers lost the variant and textual critics consistently denied its existence" (Orgel 1988: 229). In 1978, Jeanne Addison Roberts published a study that demonstrated that in the earliest prints of the first folio, Ferdinand does speak of "a wondered father and a wife" but during the course of the print run, the crossbar on the "f" broke off, turning "f" into a long "s" and erasing Miranda in the process (Roberts 1978). Despite Roberts's recovery of the original printed text, not all editors changed their minds. The 1986 Oxford edition of Shakespeare's collected works left the word as "wise." Although he acknowledges Roberts' scholarship, editor Stanley Wells insists on his own preference:

> Whereas previous critics were divided as to what F actually read, almost all preferred 'wise' as the more convincing reading. F's para-rhyme is suspicious; *wise/paradise* is a Shakespearean rhyme. 'Wife' gives trite sense and demands two grammatical licences: that 'So rare a wondered' is extended to qualify 'a wife,' and that 'Makes' has a plural subject.
>
> (Wells 1987: 616)

Regardless of the Oxford reading's details, which do more to reveal the idiosyncratic logic behind editorial quibbling than to prove its legitimacy, this wife/wise debate exposes the impossibility of readily obtaining Shakespeare's "real" text. Even if we were to have access to that fetishized point of origin, Shakespeare's fair papers in his own hand, we would still be faced with an indeterminate text, one whose literal words remained elusive to our twenty-first century eyes.[4] In noting that Roberts was able to see what earlier bibliographers missed, even when examining the same folio copies, Orgel remarks, "We find only what we are looking for or are willing to see" (Orgel 1988: 229). Although we do not often choose to acknowledge it, "Like performances, texts produce the work as an event in time" (Worthen 1997: 13) and are shaped by the same personal foibles. Neither can be said to carry the immanent meaning of the play.

Understanding both text and performance as transient alters the relationship between the two. Typically, they exist in a hierarchical dichotomy. Literary scholars see Shakespeare's meaning as contained in the text and elucidated through performance; theatre scholars prioritize performance as the source of meaning and believe the text is incomplete until it is acted on stage. Although this might sound like a balanced equation, both sides prioritize a literary notion of text. The page and the stage proponents both assume that Shakespeare's meaning is stable and that it is accessed through the text that has been transmitted to us from his hands. As W. B. Worthen points out, such assumptions limit the possibilities of Shakespearean performance by reifying discovery over interpretation (1997: 1–43). Shakespeare's meaning is valued over individual sense. The belief in a stable, timeless text is complicit in this valuing by allowing interpretations to be anchored in Shakespeare; because we believe our texts can be traced back to the author himself, we look to him to locate the meaning of the plays. But if texts are the products of their local environments, they cannot provide access to Shakespeare. We must rely on interpretation, not discovery.

The belief that the text is the means of measuring a performance is so commonplace as to seem entirely obvious. How would one approach performed Shakespeare if not through the text? The answer is through the act of performance. In companies such as the Royal Shakespeare Company, which strives to present neutral and universal realizations, it can be hard to recognize the theatrical work embedded in the presentation of a play. But desire for neutrality should not blind us to the specificity of performance. As Mazer's production of *Two Gentlemen* illustrates, sometimes the least universal aspects of theatre are the ones that make the plays speak to us most directly. The desire to see performances of Shakespeare as attesting to his universal appeal assumes that it is Shakespeare's lines that are making the theatre reverberate. But the "deeply human presences" that Verlyn Klinkenborg finds in the plays and in our fireside chats about the playwright (Klinkenborg 1999: A14) come not from Shakespeare's transcendent knowledge of humanity nor his ability to encompass past, present and future. Shakespeare's lines are never irrelevant, but neither is the role of actors and directors in bringing those lines forward and giving them voice. His words are made to speak to us by the actors who say them, repeatedly, in a series of localized productions. Placing the language of theatre alongside the language of Shakespeare, we discover that we are Shakespeare, not because he describes who we are, but because we describe our many selves in the process of staging his plays.

Notes

Introduction: Local habitations

1 As these recent books show, appropriation of Shakespeare is not limited either to distant or recent times: Michael Dobson's *The Making of the National Poet* (1992) looks at Shakespeare's transformation and adaptation during the Restoration; Michael Bristol's *Shakespeare's America, America's Shakespeare* (1990) focuses on the transformation of Shakespeare into an American author; Jean Marsden's collection *The Appropriation of Shakespeare* (1991) examines post-Renaissance appropriations of the playwright for a variety of purposes, as does Christy Desmet and Robert Sawyer's volume on *Shakespeare and Appropriation* (1999); Gary Taylor's *Reinventing Shakespeare* (1989) gives an overview of the manifestations of Shakespeare and his plays from his death until now; Terence Hawkes' *Meaning by Shakespeare* (1992) argues that every age uses Shakespeare to create its own meanings; and John Joughin's collection *Shakespeare and National Culture* (1997) covers a range of nations and their uses of Shakespeare. For the importance of the history plays to the RSC identity, see Sinfield (1985).

2 After John Major announced the new National Curriculum for English in 1992, Shakespeare's role in the schools became a matter of public debate. A letter signed by twenty-one professors objecting to the new secondary school requirements was published in the *Times Higher Education Supplement* (20 November 1992); it was subsequently signed by a further 500 teachers and reprinted in the *THES* (11 June 1993). John Major responded publicly to the letter at the 1993 Conservative Party conference (Wintour and Bates 1993). See Barker (1997), Holderness and Murphy (1997) and Sinfield

(1994) for discussions of the British curriculum debate. *The Shakespeare File*, published in 1996, claimed that of the seventy prominent American colleges and universities surveyed, only twenty-three required English majors to take a Shakespeare course (Martin 1996). The National Alumni Forum's report garnered widespread coverage in American media (for a sample, see Honan 1996 and Magner 1997); only a few writers questioned the assumptions of the report (Chu 1997, Pollitt 1997 and Wilson 1997).

3   These films of the plays are: Kenneth Branagh's *Henry V* (1989), Franco Zeffirelli's *Hamlet* (1990), Christine Edzard's *As You Like It* (1992), Branagh's *Much Ado About Nothing* (1993), Oliver Parker's *Othello* (1995), Richard Loncraine's *Richard III* (1995), Branagh's *Hamlet* (1996), Adrian Noble's *A Midsummer Night's Dream* (1996), Baz Luhrmann's *Romeo + Juliet* (1996), Trevor Nunn's *Twelfth Night* (1996), Michael Hoffman's *A Midsummer Night's Dream* (1999), Julie Taymor's *Titus* (1999), Michael Almeyreda's *Hamlet* (2000) and Kenneth Branagh's *Love's Labours Lost* (2000). Filmed adaptations of the plays are: William Reilly's *Men of Respect* (1989 – *Macbeth*), Tom Stoppard's *Rosencrantz and Guildenstern are Dead* (1990 – *Hamlet*), Gus Van Sant's *My Own Private Idaho* (1991 – *1* and *2 Henry IV*), Peter Greenaway's *Prospero's Books* (1991 – *Tempest*), Anthony Drazen's *Zebrahead* (1992 – *Romeo and Juliet*), Lloyd Kaufmann's *Tromeo and Juliet* (1996 – *Romeo and Juliet*), Jocelyn Moorhouse's *A Thousand Acres* (1996 – based on Jane Smiley's adaptation of *King Lear*), Gil Junger's *10 Things I Hate About You* (1999 – *Taming of the Shrew*) and Andrezj Bartkowiak's *Romeo Must Die* (2000 – *Romeo and Juliet*). There have also been two documentaries about the plays (Mark Olshaker's 1990 *Discovering Hamlet* and Al Pacino's 1996 *Looking for Richard*) and two films about Shakespeare (Paul Schrader's 1994 *Witch Hunt* and John Madden's 1999 *Shakespeare in Love*). I have not included the scores of recent films that have included performances of or references to Shakespeare's plays.

4   For the relationship of Branagh's *Henry V* to movies about Vietnam, see Breight 1991, Bristol 1996: 97–101, Fitter 1991: 270, 273–4 and Hedrick 1997.

5   And some very clever promotional work. MTV rebroadcast the television series *My So-called Life*, which starred Claire Danes, and showed frequent promotional clips of and advertisements for the movie. Baz Luhrmann's sleeper hit, *Strictly Ballroom*, also drew in audiences to *Romeo + Juliet*. See Richard Burt (1998: 3–5 and *passim*) for the film's marketing to teen audiences. See also James Loehlin (2000) for the movie's destabilization of the teen flick genre through a postmodern aestethic and Barbara Hodgdon (1999) for the film's participation in a popular, commercial culture.

6   Cher is not the only one who thinks so. See Barbara Hodgdon (1994: 282–93) for an example of an academic reading of the impact of Mel Gibson's body.

7   Splits between Best Picture and Best Director are fairly rare in recent

Oscar history – it has happened only five times in the last forty years – and the division this time was taken to be particularly revealing. Rival film companies saw *Shakespeare in Love*'s Oscar success as due to Miramax's lavish advertising budget and not the film's intrinsic merits. Joe Roth's suggestion that women voted for the film was part of his rebuttal against the accusations that Disney (which owns Miramax) and Miramax were not playing fairly.

8 There were many other oddities about the 1999 Oscars, including the fact that Geoffrey Rush, nominated for Best Supporting Actor for his role as Henslowe in *Shakespeare in Love*, could easily have been nominated for his role as Walsingham in *Elizabeth*, and that Judi Dench, who played Elizabeth in *Shakespeare in Love*, and Cate Blanchett, who played Elizabeth in *Elizabeth*, were both nominated for Oscars. Rush, of course, was not the only cross-over actor: Joseph Fiennes played the heroines' love interest in both films, as Dudley to Blanchett's Elizabeth and Shakespeare to Paltrow's Viola.

9 I am of course here talking about the fictional Shakespeare of the movie, and not the historical Shakespeare. Aside from the much vaunted questions about Shakespeare's sexuality, most early modern men were likely to operate through much more fluid categories than the twentieth-century dichotomy of heterosexual/homosexual. In this aspect, Shakespeare and his contemporaries were indeed queer by modern standards.

10 This tendency to attribute all good things in the film to Tom Stoppard's skill and to lay the blame for all bad things at the feet of Marc Norman – or to deny Norman any credit for the screenplay's wittiness – is a move that many of the film's reviewers made. None of them, however, comment on how this replicates the controversies over Shakespeare's own collaborations with fellow playwrights and critics' subsequent strategies in trying to determine who wrote what.

11 In addition to the scholarship on Branagh's *Henry V* that has already been cited, see Lisa Starks on Branagh's deeply Oedipal *Hamlet* (Starks 1999).

12 It is always difficult, when writing about feminist performance, to define precisely what that term encompasses. As will become apparent during the course of my book, definitions of what is or is not feminist shift for every speaker and listener – each of the following chapters touches on the debate of what is allowable for Shakespeare and what is allowable for feminism. For my purposes, the broadest definition is the best: I use "feminist" to refer to those actors, directors, and performances which strive to question received assumptions about Shakespeare's depiction of and appropriate-ness for women. The precise meaning of the word will change in each occurrence, reflecting the continual contest over the relationship between women, Shakespeare, and ideology.

1 The ideologies of acting and the performances of women

1 Berry and Rodenburg are far from the only influential voice teachers around. Kristin Linklater's two texts on voice, *Freeing the Natural Voice* and *Freeing Shakespeare's Voice*, are equally popular, particularly in North America, and the actors and teachers she has trained through her appointment at Emerson College and her work with Shakespeare and Co. and Company of Women have made her an influential teacher. But while Linklater is an important figure in late twentieth-century voice work in America, Berry and Rodenburg's connection to the RSC make them foundational figures in our examination of the RSC's performance practices. Linklater's voice work also differs significantly from Berry's and Rodenburg's in theory and application and cannot fully be addressed within the context of the RSC or even Shakespeare.

2 In her foreword to Jacqueline Martin's history of voice in modern theatre, Berry comments that the current emphasis on a naturalness of speech has thrown off both actors and audiences when they come to Shakespeare. Audiences, she claims, are ambivalent about how the plays should sound: "they want it to sound like Shakespeare but they also want it to sound like everyday speech – they want both rhetoric and simplicity" (Martin 1991: xvii). Voice work not only gives actors a way of balancing these two demands, it helps audiences to recognize the right way to hear Shakespeare.

3 For information about the history of voice work, see Martin 1991, Mennen 1997 and Acker 1997; for more on Berry's relationship to Brook, see Knowles 1996: 93–5.

4 Although voice work's roots are clearly British, it does have a strong American strain built into it. Berry attributes her development of voice work in part to her American husband's Method training (Parker 1985: 32 and Berry 1992: 288).

5 These assumptions emerge despite their authors' stated interest in political activism and individual agency. Berry believes in having "a commitment to the work beyond a personal commitment, which is to do with seeing theatre as a serious political force in the context of the society we live in" (Berry 1992: 21). But in her view, the power of theatre to effect change has largely to do with the actor's commitment to the author's words, not the actor's challenge to those words. Berry repeatedly speaks of honoring the text – its meaning, rhythm, texture (Berry 1992: 25, 27, 30, 52, 65, 78, 157, 178) – and insists that to do otherwise will render it unintelligible. While trusting the actor to deliver and the audience to receive a story's lessons, she does not leave room for the actor to challenge the story itself. Shakespeare stays beyond judgement, a source of political power but not an object of political reproach. More explicitly than Berry, Rodenburg couches her work in political language, but she too ultimately backs away from political action. The right to speak, she argues, is a powerful one with

potentially great ramifications and she is continually sensitive to the ways in which gender, race and class are political forces that affect how we use our voices and language. But while Rodenburg pays extended attention to the cultural politics of speech, she finally argues that it is not necessary to change the underlying reasons for bad vocal habits in order to recover the right to speak: "It is very useful to understand some of the ultimate causes of any debilitating or even mildly irritating habit, but often just releasing the physical tension that has found its way into the voice by whatever means will be sufficient" (Rodenburg 1992: 27). The emphasis that Rodenburg repeatedly places on the need to give yourself the right to speak (or the right to breathe, or the right to judge yourself, or any of the other many rights that she exhorts her readers to claim) undermines her call for societal change and turns political repression into an internalized problem.

6 Even early modern male actors would have been unlikely to achieve the sort of Stanislavskian becoming of character that today's actors generally strive for. For an account of the distance between the modern ethos of acting and Renaissance notions of personation, see Joseph Roach's *The Player's Passion* (1985).

7 There are certainly ways to block a scene so as to disrupt this pattern of focusing on the action instead of the reaction. In a 1985 production of the play directed by Michael Bogdanov at Stratford, Ontario, Angelo's face was turned away from the audience while he groped at Isabella, leaving the audience to look at her face and focus on her reaction to his mimed orgasm. In this case, Isabella's paralysis had a great amount of performative power. But unless the director deliberately leads the audience's attention to the reaction, the center of attention tends to remain on the active character (in film there is a camera angle referred to as a "reaction shot" but no term for the more common action shot).

8 Hodgdon follows her analysis of Leavis' performed reading of *Othello* with a critique of Ian McKellen's reading of his performance as Macbeth in 1979 that makes similar observations to the ones I make here about the relationship between Shakespeare's meaning and the actor's body. Although she is not considering the specific rubric of voice work, much of McKellen's methodology draws on the work of Berry (Hodgdon 1994: 264–75).

9 This scrupulous attention to detail also opens up theatre practitioners to academic ridicule, for all too often they fail to take into account the historical conditions of printing and textual variation that make up what they want to read as a uniform script created solely by Shakespeare. *King Lear* and *Hamlet* are spoken of in the voice texts as if they were single entities, with no acknowledgment of their various folio and quarto versions; punctuation and line-endings are seen as indicators of Shakespeare's intent without acknowledgment of the role copy editors and typesetters played in the printing of the texts. This misreading of Renaissance printing practices

is particularly extreme in the reverence shown to the First Folio as the playscript that contains all of Shakespeare's performance clues; see Kristin Linklater's tribute to Neil Freeman's Folio scripts (Linklater 1992: 204–7). Janette Dillon's critique of editors' attempts to recreate an original Shakespearean performance from early quartos is also a useful critique of theatre practitioners' desire to read printed texts as accurate records of Renaissance material practices of performance (Dillon 1994).

10   This institutional tension between the theatre and academics is one of the reasons that theatre historians and theatre practitioners have a notoriously troubled relationship. Particularly around the issue of feminism, historians and practitioners are often unable to speak to each other in constructive ways. My own exchange with Berry, Rodenburg and Kristin Linklater in *New Theatre Quarterly* is an apt example of how this is played out (Werner 1996, Berry 1997b, Werner 1997). Jane Boston picks up on the way in which we speak different languages: practitioners' use of metaphorical descriptions of the acting process are too easily read by academics as literal accounts of essentialist beliefs (Boston 1997: 250), while academics' efforts to analyze theatre practice are too easily dismissed by practitioners as academic, and not practical. Certainly in this instance, my desire to discuss ideological structures was misheard by the voice coaches as accusations that they themselves were not good feminists; their response was not to address the historicist and ideological issues I had raised, but to wonder why I endorsed "inorganic and untrue" performances and whether I had ever bothered to work on my own voice (Berry 1997b: 52, 49). Instead of a constructive conversation, participants speak past each other, with only the rare exceptions who have a foot in both camps, like Jane Boston and Ellen O'Brien (1998), able to address both sides of the debate. But even academic practitioners have trouble communicating with practitioners who are employed outside of universities; Lizbeth Goodman, in a private conversation, has suggested that much of the problem stems from the discrepancy in compensation, with feminist performers and directors outside of academia jealous of the resources and steady employment enjoyed by feminist university lecturers and professors. The ramifications of the institutional tensions that I have outlined affect not only the past development of voice work, but the continuing practice of theatre.

11   Although Andrew Wade has taken over the position of Head Voice Coach at the RSC since Berry's retirement, he has yet to make a significant impact on the tradition of voice training.

12   Not all directors, of course, are university educated. But the RSC has long been dominated by directors who come out of university rather than acting or stage management.

13   Aside from my own earlier article on voice work (Werner 1996), no one else has addressed this aspect of voice work. The rare exceptions who even mention Berry are Douglas Lanier, who includes Berry along with Barton

in his discussion of the textual scrutiny methods of the RSC (Lanier 1996: 189), and W. B. Worthen, who examines Berry along with other voice teachers in his discussion of acting books (Worthen 1997: 95–125). Lanier's, Worthen's and my own article all postdate Knowles' original manuscript and, with the exception of Lanier, clearly build on the work that Knowles has done.

2   Punching Daddy, or the politics of company politics

1   My research would not have been possible without the willingness of Terry Hands, Genista McIntosh, Fiona Shaw and Susan Lily Todd to be interviewed about their experience of the Women's Group, and I am grateful to them for making room for me in their busy schedules. I have been unable to track down or arrange interviews with other participants in the Group's history, making the contributions of those who could participate all the more important and generous. The librarians at the Shakespeare Centre were indispensable for their help in pursuing the group's history through the Centre's archives. But the person I am most indebted to is Lizbeth Goodman, whose early published account of the Group gave me the first hint of their existence, who generously gave me her press file on *Heresies* and who spoke with me about her experiences researching the group. Without Goodman's research and encouragement, the RSC Women's Group could have easily remained hidden.

2   Unless otherwise noted, all quotes in this chapter from Fiona Shaw, Terry Hands, Genista McIntosh and Susan Lily Todd are from my interviews with them.

3   Shaw and Stevenson have both discussed this production in a number of publications (Rutter 1988: 97–121, Shaw 1988: 55–71); Penny Gay also gives an account of the production and their roles (Gay 1994: 75–82).

4   All articles about and reviews of the RSC Women's Group and the projects leading up to it have come from the collections of Genista McIntosh and Lizbeth Goodman, and from the press clippings archived in the Shakespeare Centre; none of the press clippings have page numbers for the articles. Many of the reviews, however, can be found in the *London Theatre Record* (see volume 6 issue 25/6 and volume 7 issue 1).

5   Irene Hentschel directed *Twelfth Night* in 1939, Dorothy Green directed *A Winter's Tale* in 1943 and *Henry V* in 1946, and Margaret Webster directed *Merchant of Venice* in 1956. See Elizabeth Schafer (1998: 191–241) for a history of women directing Shakespeare in Britain. Peter Hall offered Joan Littlewood a chance to direct *1 Henry IV*, but she withdrew after he refused to allow her to cast Zero Mostel, who was blacklisted for standing as godfather to Paul Robeson's son (Schafer 1998: 231).

6   The plays Goodbody directed at the RSC were *Arden of Faversham* (Theatregoround, April 1970), *King John* (Theatregoround, June 1970),

Occupations (national tour, September 1971), *The Oz Trial* (The Place (London), November 1971), *As You Like It* (Royal Shakespeare Theatre, June 1973), *King Lear* (The Other Place, April 1974) and *Hamlet* (national tour, April 1975). She started with the company as an assistant to Terry Hands in 1968 on his *Merry Wives of Windsor*, and continued as Trevor Nunn's assistant on his 1970 *Henry VIII*, his 1972 *Antony and Cleopatra*, *Julius Caesar* and *Titus Andronicus*, and his 1973 *Coriolanus*. For more on Goodbody's career, see Callaghan 1991 and Chambers 1980.

7 Penny Cherns directed a production of Pam Gems' *Queen Christina* in 1977 in The Other Place; Sheila Hancock directed *A Midsummer Night's Dream* for the 1983 tour; Di Trevis directed *The Taming of the Shrew* and co-directed *Happy End* for the 1985 tour; Gillian Lynne co-directed *Once in a Lifetime* with Trevor Nunn in 1979 and *La Ronde* with John Barton in 1982.

8 This interview, published in April 1986, is not in the Shakespeare Centre's RSC archives, although the archives do have a clipping from *Stage and Television Today* discussing the interview and the actors' subsequent reprimand. I have in fact been unable to track down the existence of the magazine the actors spoke to, let alone a copy of their interview. Although *Stage and Television Today* reports the title of the journal as *Theatregoer Magazine*, there is no history of a publication under that name in Britain. There is an American newsletter with that title, but although I searched through the archives at the New York Public Library, I did not find mention of the interview. It seems unlikely that the American magazine is the one in question, as Shaw clearly remembers the interview being published in a glossy, widely-read industry magazine. I have looked through back issues of a number of such journals, but have not as yet found the interview.

9 For a history of feminist theatre in Britain, see Goodman 1993a and Wandor 1986; see also Goodman's collection of interviews with women in mainstream and fringe theatre (Goodman 1996).

10 This was not the first time a woman at the RSC wanted to work on *Macbeth* only to be told that it wasn't appropriate. Di Trevis recalls a similar experience in the early 1980s when she was interviewing to be Terry Hands' assistant: "I wanted desperately to do *Macbeth* and I didn't want to do 'a woman's play', not because they didn't interest me but because I felt that everybody expected it. I can't describe to you how there were underlying assumptions in those days and everybody would expect you to do an *As You Like It* or a *Twelfth Night*. When I was interviewed to be Terry Hands' assistant at the RSC, I said that the play that interested me was *Henry V* and they just went 'Oh!!!' and they absolutely didn't want me to do *Macbeth*" (Schafer 1998: 162–3).

11 Susan Carlson, who interviewed Wertenbaker on 3 May 1986, writes that Wertenbaker "turned down an offer to write for [the RSC Women's Group], having envisioned that the tensions of collaborative work in the

subsidized theatre would be exaggerated there" (Carlson 1991: 288). I have not interviewed Wertenbaker, but this reasoning as stated by Carlson would not be incompatible with Todd's assessment of her departure. The date of Carlson's interview suggests that the time frame Todd recollects for the group is slightly inaccurate.

12 The women who directed at the company until 1986 were Buzz Goodbody, Penny Cherns, Gillian Lynne (who co-directed with male directors), Sheila Hancock, Alison Sutcliffe, Di Trevis and Susan Todd. After *Heresies*, the women directing at the RSC were Deborah Warner, Di Trevis, Jude Kelly, Sarah Pia Anderson, Cicely Berry, Garry Hynes, Janice Honeyman, Janet Suzman, Phyllida Lloyd, Katie Mitchell and Gale Edwards. Lynne Parker and Simona Gonella will direct in the 2000/01 season. I have only included those women who directed shows as part of the main company, not those who directed at the associated festivals or at the theatres as part of outside productions.

13 See Jennie Long's 1994 follow-up to the Women's Playhouse Trust survey (Long 1994) and my own article on the report (Werner 1998).

3 *The Taming of the Shrew*: A case study in performance criticism

1 It is partly in reaction to the play's continual erasure of its heroine's subjectivity that I insist on calling her Katherine, the name that she chooses for herself ("They call me Katherine that do talk of me" (2.1.182)), rather than the more familiar Kate, the name that Petruchio insists on during his taming.

2 The fullness of these restorations still remained at some distance from the Folio text. J. R. Planché and Benjamin Webster's 1844 production did use most of the Folio text, including the Induction, although some particularly bawdy lines were cut. Augustin Daly's 1877 production, despite his claims of textual purity, cut almost a third of Shakespeare's words and used some of Garrick's changes to the wooing and submission scenes. See Tori Haring-Smith (1985: 43–72) for a detailed account of these productions.

3 For a history of *Shrew* on stage see Tori Haring-Smith (1985), Ann Thompson (1984: 17–24), Graham Holderness (1989) and Penny Gay (1994: 86–119). Barbara Hodgdon (1998: 1–38) and Diana Henderson (1998) discuss films of *Shrew* particularly in terms of their relationship to gender ideology. Carol Rutter (1989: 1–25) has discussions by three actors who played Katherine at the RSC and Elizabeth Schafer (1998: 57–72) looks at productions of the play directed by women.

4 Ann Thompson concludes her introduction to the play, "I suspect we shall have to acknowledge that we can no longer treat *The Shrew* as a straightforward comedy but must redefine it as a problem play in Ernest Schanzer's sense: 'A play in which we find a concern with a moral problem which is central to it, presented in such a manner that we are unsure of our

moral bearings, so that uncertain and divided responses to it in the minds of the audience are possible or even probable' " (Thompson 1984: 41).

5 Boose accomplishes much the same effect in her earlier *Shrew* article, which focused on scold's bridles in order to excavate the play's intertextual history (Boose 1991). Both pieces are explicitly set up as feminist readings that circumvent the desire to find comic fulfillment in the play, and both illuminate both the material culture from which *Shrew* emerged and the modern demands and benefits of acknowledging that ideology.

6 Edwards' production of *Shrew* followed Buzz Goodbody's 1973 *As You Like It* and Di Trevis' 1988 *Much Ado About Nothing* at the Royal Shakespeare Theatre; Trevis directed a touring production of *Shrew* in 1985. The five productions of *Shrew* in the thirteen-year interval were Barry Kyle's in 1982, Trevis' in 1985, Jonathan Miller's in 1987, Bill Alexander's in 1990 for the national tour and revived in 1992 for the main stage, and Edwards' in 1995; this does not include Adrian Noble's *Kiss Me Kate* in 1987, which made for the unusual back-to-back *Shrews* in Stratford that year.

7 See Lynda Boose for the relationship between Katherine's speech and early sixteenth-century marriage sermons and the speech's construction as a nostalgic reordering of societal structure (1991: 182–3 and 1994: 195–6).

8 Graham Holderness writes about the way in which the tourism of Stratford-upon-Avon participates in the "Shakespeare myth" (Holderness 1988). See also Hodgdon 1998: 191–240.

9 Bogdanov's was perhaps the most influential production of *Shrew* in the late twentieth century. For more on his production from the participants' point of view, see Bogdanov's interview with Christopher McCullough (McCullough 1988c) and Paola Dionisotti's account of playing Katherine in that production (Rutter 1989: 1–4, 22–23). Graham Holderness discusses the production in his stage history of *Shrew* (1989: 73–94); Penny Gay also includes it in her feminist stage history of the comedies (1994: 104–11). Gay's discussion is particularly useful for the distinction she makes between those reviewers who were sensitive to the production's gender critique and those who responded solely to the farcical elements and Jonathan Pryce's star power as Petruchio.

10 Not every audience reacted the same way: the second time I saw the play, at a matinee a month later, the audience did not applaud their kiss. Regardless of the frequency of such applause, it suggests audiences came to the play expecting to see a romantic comedy and wanting that expectation to be fulfilled.

11 Ann Thompson, for instance, quotes Shaw in her Cambridge edition of the play (1984: 21), as does Brian Morris in his Arden edition (1981: 144), Barbara Hodgdon quotes this passage in her examination of *Shrew* (1998: 28) and Michael Billington refers to Shaw in his review of Edwards' *Shrew* (1995). Shaw's 6 November 1897 *Saturday Review* article, however, is far from a straightforward condemnation of the gender politics of the play.

While he is uncomfortable by Katherine's final speech, he enjoys the taming itself: "The process is quite bearable, because the selfishness of the man is healthily goodhumored and untainted by wanton cruelty, and it is good for the shrew to encounter a force like that and be brought to her senses" (Wilson 1961: 188). Shaw is often quoted as evidence of his dislike of the play's gender politics, but it is also possible to read his reaction as stemming from the discomfort of watching Katherine's submission "in the company of a woman" – perhaps his enjoyment of the moment is stifled by not being in the safety of a men's club.

12 All reviews of this production are quoted from the press clippings archived at the Shakespeare Centre; page numbers are not retained in the clippings.

13 This is precisely the point that Shirley Garner makes in her article, "*The Taming of the Shrew*: Inside or Outside the Joke?" (Garner 1988). Examining the question of whether *Shrew* can be considered a farce, she writes, "Accepting it for the moment as farce, I would ask rather: Could the taming of a 'shrew' be considered the proper subject of farce in any but a misogynist culture? How would we feel about a play entitled *The Taming of the Jew* or *The Taming of the Black*?" (1988: 109). Garner is too quick to collapse women, Jews and blacks into one group of "the oppressed" and I would argue that all three continue to be written into today's taming stories. But her question of who is inside the joke remains a helpful articulation of how *Shrew* works.

14 A number of academics have written about this production. Some praised its handling of gender relationships and its ability to create a new framework and meaning for the play separate from the traditional Shakespearean script (Gay 1999, Hodgdon 1998: 30–8, Holland 1997: 236–40). Others were more skeptical about the textual changes, like the reviewers, but managed to ask questions about the implications of such changes without relying on the misogynistic assumptions found in the newspapers (Dessen 1996: 7–8, Jackson 1996: 324–6). On the other hand, some of the newspaper reviewers praised Edwards' gender politics and described them as one of the strengths of the production (de Jongh 1995, Doughty 1995, Tinker 1995). Although it is possible to group these viewers into communities that might account for their readings (Dessen and Jackson were reviewing for Shakespeare journals, Doughty was the one female reviewer for the national papers), these rearrangements fail to cohere completely (Holland was also writing for a Shakespeare journal and de Jongh and Tinker were male reviewers praising Edwards' politics).

15 Prioritizing actors' accounts of their performances is, of course, an ideologically inflected decision. See Worthen (1997: 95–150).

Epilogue: The language of theatre

1 The issue of Silvia's reaction to the assault and to Valentine's offer to give her to Proteus was left unfixed. Some nights Silvia (or rather, the frame character playing Silvia) accepted the attempts made by the frame character playing Julia to comfort her. Most nights, according to Mazer, Silvia was unable to be comforted and remained isolated from the rest of the women on stage.

2 Penn, like most undergraduate acting programs, has many more women than men as majors. As a result, most college and university productions rely heavily on cross-casting and on finding plays that offer many roles for women. Conservatories, particularly those that focus on classical theatre, often limit the number of women admitted to the program so as to create a ratio of male to female parts that more closely mirrors what is offered in classical drama.

3 Unless otherwise indicated, all quotes from Mazer are from my interview of him.

4 For a sense of the instability of the material text, see Margreta de Grazia and Peter Stallybrass (1993). W. B. Worthen gives a good overview of recent editorial theory and its relationship to performance (1997: 1–43). Leah Marcus, in her recent work on editing Elizabeth I's papers, argues convincingly that the fantasy of Shakespeare's handwriting resolving questions of textual cruxes is an impossible one (2000).

Bibliography

Acker, Barbara (1997) " 'I Charge Thee Speak': John Barrymore and his Voice Coach, Margaret Carrington," in Marion Hampton and Barbara Acker (eds), *The Vocal Vision: Views on Voice by 24 Leading Teachers, Coaches and Directors*, New York and London: Applause, 143–54.

Alderson, Kate (1995) "Whose shrew is it anyway?" *The Times*, 21 April.

Barber, Frances (1988) "Ophelia in *Hamlet*," in Russell Jackson and Robert Smallwood (eds), *Players of Shakespeare 2: Further Essays in Shakespearean Performance by Players with the Royal Shakespeare Company*, Cambridge: Cambridge University Press, 137–50.

Barker, Simon (1997) "Re-loading the Canon: Shakespeare and the Study Guides," in John J. Joughin (ed.), *Shakespeare and National Culture*, Manchester: Manchester University Press, 42–57.

Barton, John (1984) *Playing Shakespeare*, London and New York: Methuen.

Beauman, Sally (1982) *The Royal Shakespeare Company: A History of Ten Decades*, Oxford: Oxford University Press.

Belsey, Catherine (1985) *The Subject of Tragedy: Identity and Difference in Renaissance Drama*, London and New York: Methuen.

Bennett, Kenneth C. (1999) Letter to the Editor, *New York Times*, 12 February, A26.

Berry, Cicely (1973) *Voice and the Actor*, London: Harrap.

—— (1987) *The Actor and His Text*, London: Harrap.

—— (1992) *The Actor and The Text*, Second Edition, London: Virgin Books.

—— (1997) "Speaking the Speech," in Stanley Wells (ed.), *Summerfolk: A Celebration: Fifty Years of Shakespeare and the Stratford Theatres*, Ebrington, Gloucestershire: Long Barn Books, 91–8.

Berry, Cicely, Patsy Rodenburg and Kristin Linklater (1997) "Shakespeare, Feminism, and Voice: Responses to Sarah Werner," *New Theatre Quarterly* 49: 48–52.

Berry, Ralph (1985) "The Reviewer as Historian," *Shakespeare Quarterly* 36: 594–7.

Billington, Michael (1993) *One Night Stands: A Critic's View of British Theatre from 1971–1991*, London: Nick Hern Books.

—— (1995) Review of *The Taming of the Shrew*, *Guardian*, 24 April.

Bloom, Harold (1998) *Shakespeare: The Invention of the Human*, New York: Riverhead Books.

Boose, Lynda (1991) "Scolding Brides and Bridling Scolds: Taming the Woman's Unruly Member," *Shakespeare Quarterly* 42: 179–213.

—— (1994) "*The Taming of the Shrew*, Good Husbandry, and Enclosure," in Russ McDonald (ed.), *Shakespeare Reread: The Texts in New Contexts*, Ithaca, NY and London: Cornell University Press, 193–225.

Boston, Jane (1995) Interview with the author, Brighton, Sussex, 27 February.

—— (1997) "Voice, the Practitioners, their Practices, and their Critics," *New Theatre Quarterly* 51: 248–54.

Branagh, Kenneth (1989) dir. *Henry V*, with Kenneth Branagh, Derek Jacobi and Emma Thompson, Renaissance Films.

Breight, Curtis (1991) "Branagh and the Prince, or a Royal Fellowship of Death," *Critical Quarterly* 33: 95–111.

Bristol, Michael D. (1996) *Big-time Shakespeare*, London and New York: Routledge.

—— (1990) *Shakespeare's America, America's Shakespeare*, London and New York: Routledge.

Brook, Peter (1968) *The Empty Space*, New York: Atheneum.

Bulman, James C. (1996) "Introduction: Shakespeare and Performance Theory," in James C. Bulman (ed.), *Shakespeare, Theory, and Performance*, London and New York: Routledge, 1–11.

Burns, Edward (1990) *Character: Acting and Being on the Pre-Modern Stage*, London: Macmillan.

Burt, Richard (1998) *Unspeakable ShaXXXspeares: Queer Theory and American Kiddie Culture*, New York: St Martin's Press.

Callaghan, Dympna (1991) "Buzz Goodbody: Directing for Change," in Jean I. Marsden (ed.), *The Appropriation of Shakespeare: Post-Renaissance Reconstructions of the Works and the Myth*, Hemel Hempstead, Hertfordshire: Harvester Wheatsheaf, 163–81.

Carlson, Susan (1991) *Women and Comedy: Rewriting the British Theatrical Tradition*, Ann Arbor: University of Michigan Press.

—— (1998) "The Suffrage Shrew: The Shakespeare Festival, 'A Man's Play,' and New Women," in Jonathan Bate, Jill L. Levenson and Dieter Mehl (eds), *Shakespeare and the Twentieth Century: The Selected Proceedings of the International*

Shakespeare Association World Congress, Los Angeles, 1996, Newark: University of Delaware Press, 85–102.

Case, Sue-Ellen (1988) *Feminism and Theatre*, New York: Methuen.

Chambers, Colin (1980) *Other Spaces: New Theatre and the RSC*, London: Eyre Methuen and TQ Publications.

Chu, Henry (1997) "Reports of the Bard's Demise are Premature," *Los Angeles Times*, 25 March, A1.

Cork, Sir Kenneth, chairman (1986) *Theatre Is for All: Report of the Enquiry into Professional Theatre in England*, London: Arts Council of Great Britain.

Cornwell, Jane (1995) "An Australian in Stratford," *Southern Cross*, 19 April.

Coveney, Michael (1995) Review of *The Taming of the Shrew*, *Observer*, 23 April.

Cowell, Stephanie (1999) "*Shakespeare in Love*," *Shakespeare: A Magazine for Teachers and Enthusiasts*. Online. Available: http://www.shakespearemag.com/reviews/shakespeareinlove.asp (18 October 1999).

Dachslager, Earl L. (1999) Letter to the Editor, *New York Times*, 12 February, A26.

de Grazia, Margreta and Peter Stallybrass (1993) "The Materiality of the Shakespearean Text," *Shakespeare Quarterly* 44: 255–83.

de Jongh, Nicholas (1995) Review of *The Taming of the Shrew*, *Evening Standard*, 24 April.

Desmet, Christy and Robert Sawyer (eds) (1999) *Shakespeare and Appropriation*, London and New York: Routledge.

Dessen, Alan (1996) "Improving the Script: Staging Shakespeare and Others in 1995," *Shakespeare Bulletin* 14 (Winter): 5–8.

Dillon, Janette (1994) "Is There a Performance in this Text?" *Shakespeare Quarterly* 45: 74–86.

Dobson, Michael (1992) *The Making of the National Poet: Shakespeare, Adaptation and Authorship, 1660–1769*, Oxford: Clarendon Press.

Doughty, Louise (1995) Review of *The Taming of the Shrew*, *Mail on Sunday*, 30 April.

Duncan-Jones, Katherine (1999) "Why, then, O brawling love!" *The Times Literary Supplement*, 5 February, 18.

Dunderdale, Sue (1984) "The Status of Women in British Theatre Survey," *Drama* 152: 9–11.

Ellis, Katherine (1999) "Why 'Shakespeare' Won," *New York Times*, 25 March, A30.

Fish, Stanley (1980) *Is There a Text in This Class?: The Authority of Interpretive Communities*, Cambridge, Massachusetts: Harvard University Press.

Fitter, Chris (1991) "A Tale of Two Branaghs: *Henry V*, Ideology, and the Mekong Agincourt," in Ivo Kamps (ed.), *Shakespeare Left and Right*, London and New York: Routledge, 259–75.

Gardiner, Caroline (1987) *What Share of the Cake? The Employment of Women in the English Theatre*, London: Women's Playhouse Trust. Excerpted in Lizbeth Goodman (ed.) with Jane de Gay, *The Routledge Reader in Gender and Performance*, London and New York: Routledge, 1998, 97–102.

Garner, Shirley (1988) "*The Taming of the Shrew*: Inside or Outside the Joke?" in Maurice Charney (ed.), *"Bad" Shakespeare: Revaluations of the Shakespeare Canon*, Rutherford, NJ: Fairleigh Dickinson University Press, 105–19.

Gay, Penny (1994) *As She Likes It: Shakespeare's Unruly Women*, London and New York: Routledge.

—— (1999) "Recent Australian *Shrews*: The 'Larrikin Element,'" in Marianne Novy (ed.), *Transforming Shakespeare: Contemporary Women's Re-Visions in Literature and Performance*, New York: St. Martin's Press, 35–50.

Goodman, Lizbeth (1993a) *Contemporary Feminist Theatres: To Each Her Own*, London and New York: Routledge.

—— (1993b) "Women's Alternative Shakespeares and Women's Alternatives to Shakespeare in Contemporary British Theater" in Marianne Novy (ed.), *Cross-Cultural Performances: Differences in Women's Re-Visions of Shakespeare*, Urbana and Chicago: University of Illinois Press, 206–26.

—— (ed.) with Jane de Gay (1996) *Feminist Stages: Interviews with Women in Contemporary British Theatre*, Amsterdam: Harwood Academic Press.

Greenblatt, Stephen (1999) "About That Romantic Sonnet . . ." *New York Times*, 6 February, A15.

Gross, John (1995) Review of *The Taming of the Shrew*, *Sunday Telegraph*, 30 April.

Hands, Terry (1996) Interview with the author, London, 18 April.

Haring-Smith, Tori (1985) *From Farce to Metadrama: A Stage History of* The Taming of the Shrew, *1594–1983*, Westport, Connecticut and London, England: Greenwood Press.

Hawkes, Terence (1992) *Meaning by Shakespeare*, London and New York: Routledge.

Heckerling, Amy (1995), dir. *Clueless*, with Alicia Silverstone and Paul Rudder, Paramount.

Hedrick, Donald K. (1997) "War is Mud: Branagh's Dirty Harry V and the Types of Political Ambiguity," in Lynda E. Boose and Richard Burt (eds), *Shakespeare, the Movie: Popularizing the Plays on Film, TV, and Video*, London and New York: Routledge, 45–66.

Helms, Lorraine (1994) "Acts of Resistance: The Feminist Player," in Dympna Callaghan, Lorraine Helms and Jyotsna Singh, *The Weyward Sisters: Shakespeare and Feminist Politics*, Oxford, UK and Cambridge, USA: Blackwell, 102–56.

Henderson, Diana (1998) "A Shrew for the Times," in Lynda Boose and Richard Burt (eds), *Shakespeare the Movie: Popularizing the Plays on Film, TV, and Video*, London and New York: Routledge, 148–68.

Hodgdon, Barbara (1994) "The Critic, the Poor Player, Prince Hamlet, and the Lady in the Dark," in Russ McDonald (ed.), *Shakespeare Reread: The Texts in New Contexts*, Ithaca, NY and London: Cornell University Press, 258–93.

—— (1998) *The Shakespeare Trade: Performances and Appropriations*, Philadelphia: University of Pennsylvania Press.

—— (1999) "*William   Shakespeare's   Romeo + Juliet*:   Everything's   Nice   in America?" *Shakespeare Survey* 52: 88–98.

Holderness, Graham (1988) "Bardolatry: or, the Cultural Materialist's Guide to Stratford-upon-Avon," in Graham Holderness (ed.), *The Shakespeare Myth*, Manchester: Manchester University Press, 2–15.

—— (1989) *The Taming of the Shrew: Shakespeare in Performance*, Manchester: Manchester University Press.

Holderness, Graham and Andrew Murphy (1997) "Shakespeare's England: Britain's Shakespeare," in John J. Joughin (ed.), *Shakespeare and National Culture*, Manchester: Manchester University Press, 19–41.

Holland, Peter (1997) *English Shakespeares: Shakespeare on the English stage in the 1990s*, Cambridge: Cambridge University Press.

Honan, William H. (1996) "Alas, Poor Shakespeare: No Longer a 'Must Read' at Many Colleges," *New York Times*, 29 December, A13.

Jackson, Russell (1996) "Shakespeare at Stratford-upon-Avon, 1995–96," *Shakespeare Quarterly* 47: 319–26.

Joughin, John (ed.) (1997) *Shakespeare and National Culture*, Manchester, UK and New York: Manchester University Press.

Kakutani, Michiko (1999) "All the World's a Stage, Ruled by Guess Who," *New York Times*, 18 March.

Kissler, Linda (1997) "Teaching Shakespeare Through Film," in Ronald E. Salomone and James E. Davis (eds), *Teaching Shakespeare into the Twenty-first Century*, Athens, Ohio: Ohio University Press, 201–7.

Klawans, Stuart (1999a) "Oscar Who?" *The Nation*, 15 March.

—— (1999b) "Two, Like, Star-crossed Lovers," *The Nation*, 22 February.

Klinkenborg, Verlyn (1999) "Warming Ourselves Beside Shakespeare's Fire," *New York Times*, 13 March, A14.

Knowles,   Richard   Paul   (1996)   "Shakespeare,   Voice,   and   Ideology: Interrogating the Natural Voice," in James C. Bulman (ed.), *Shakespeare, Theory, and Performance*, London and New York: Routledge, 92–112.

Lanier, Douglas (1996) "Drowning the Book: *Prospero's Books* and the Textual Shakespeare," in James C. Bulman (ed.), *Shakespeare, Theory, and Performance*, London and New York: Routledge, 187–209.

Linklater, Kristin (1976) *Freeing the Natural Voice*, New York: Drama Book Publishers.

—— (1992) *Freeing Shakespeare's Voice: The Actor's Guide to Talking the Text*, New York: Theatre Communications Group.

Loehlin, James N. (2000) "'These Violent Delights Have Violent Ends': Baz Luhrmann's Millennial Shakespeare," in Mark Thornton Burnett and Ramona Wray (eds), *Shakespeare, Film, Fin de Siècle*, New York: Macmillan.

Londré, Felicia with Kimberly L. Janczuk (1999) "A Guide to American Shakespeare Companies and Festivals with Academic Affiliations," in Milla Cozart Riggio (ed.), *Teaching Shakespeare through Performance*, New York: Modern Language Association, 435–41.

Long, Jennie (1994) *What Share of the Cake Now? The Employment of Women in the English Theatre*, London: Women's Playhouse Trust. Excerpted in Lizbeth Goodman (ed.) with Jane de Gay, *The Routledge Reader in Gender and Performance*, London and New York: Routledge, 1998, 103–7.

Luhrmann, Baz (1996) dir. *William Shakespeare's Romeo + Juliet*, with Leonardo DiCaprio and Claire Danes, 20th Century Fox.

Macaulay, Alistair (1995) Review of *The Taming of the Shrew*, *Financial Times*, 28 April.

McCullough, Christopher J. (1988a) "The Cambridge Connection: Towards a Materialist Theatre Practice," in Graham Holderness (ed.), *The Shakespeare Myth*, Manchester: Manchester University Press, 112–21.

—— (1988b) Interview with Terry Hands, in Graham Holderness (ed.), *The Shakespeare Myth*, Manchester: Manchester University Press, 122–7.

—— (1988c) Interview with Michael Bogdanov, in Graham Holderness (ed.), *The Shakespeare Myth*, Manchester: Manchester University Press, 89–95.

McIntosh, Genista (1995) Interview with the author, London, 17 May.

McLuskie, Kathleen (1985) "The Patriarchal Bard: Feminist Criticism and Shakespeare: *King Lear* and *Measure for Measure*," in Jonathan Dollimore and Alan Sinfield (eds), *Political Shakespeare: New Essays in Cultural Materialism*, Ithaca, NY: Cornell University Press, 88–108.

Madden, John (1999) dir. *Shakespeare in Love*, with Gwyneth Paltrow and Joseph Fiennes, Miramax Pictures.

Magner, Denise (1997) "Top English Departments No Longer Require Courses on Shakespeare, a Study Finds," *Chronicle of Higher Education*, 10 January, A12.

Manfull, Helen (1997) *In Other Words: Women Directors Speak*, Lyme, NH: Smith and Kraus.

Marcus, Leah S. (1996) *Unediting the Renaissance: Shakespeare, Marlowe, Milton*, London and New York: Routledge.

—— (2000) "The Veil of Manuscript," unpublished paper, Shakespeare Association of America, Montreal, 8 April.

Marsden, Jean (ed.) (1991) *The Appropriation of Shakespeare: Post-Renaissance Reconstructions of the Works and the Myth*, New York: Harvester Wheatsheaf.

Martin, Jacqueline (1991) *Voice in Modern Theatre*, London and New York: Routledge.

Martin, Jerry L. (1996) *The Shakespeare File: What English Majors Are Really Studying*, with Anne D. Neal and Michael S. Nadel, Washington, D.C.: National Alumni Forum.

Mazer, Cary (2000) Interview with the author, Philadelphia, 1 March.

Mennen, Dorothy Runk (1997) "Voice Training, Where Have We Come From?" in Marion Hampton and Barbara Acker (eds), *The Vocal Vision: Views on Voice by 24 Leading Teachers, Coaches and Directors*, New York and London: Applause, 123–32.

Morris, Brian (ed.) (1981) *The Taming of the Shrew*, William Shakespeare, London and New York: Methuen.

Mullin, Michael (1994) *Theatre at Stratford-upon-Avon, First Supplement: A Catalogue-Index to Productions of the Royal Shakespeare Company, 1979–1993*, Westport, Conneticut: Greenwood Press.

Neely, Carol Thomas (1985) *Broken Nuptials in Shakespeare's Plays*, New Haven and London: Yale University Press.

Nightingale, Benedict (1995) Review of *The Taming of the Shrew*, *The Times*, 24 April.

Noble, Adrian (2000) "At Age 436, His Future is Unlimited," *New York Times*, 23 April, Arts 5.

O'Brien, Ellen (1998) "Mapping the Role: Criticism and the Construction of Shakespearean Character," in Jay L. Halio and Hugh Richmond (eds), *Shakespearean Illuminations: Essays in Honor of Marvin Rosenberg*, Newark: University of Delaware Press, 13–32.

Oliver, H. J. (ed.) (1982) *The Taming of the Shrew*, William Shakespeare, Oxford: Clarendon Press.

Orgel, Stephen (1988) "Prospero's Wife," in Stephen Greenblatt (ed.), *Representing the English Renaissance*, Berkeley: University of California Press, 217–29.

Parker, Kate (1985) "Goodbye, Voice Beautiful," *Plays and Players* 382: 32–3.

Parrish, Sue (1984) *The Status of Women in the British Theatre, 1982–1983*, London: Conference of Women Theatre Directors and Administrators.

Pascal, Julia (1985) *City Limits*, 25–31 October.

Peter, John (1995) Review of *The Taming of the Shrew*, *Sunday Times*, 30 April.

Pollitt, Katha (1997) "Sweet Swan of Avon!" *The Nation*, 4 March, 9.

Rackin, Phyllis (1998) "Dating Shakespeare's Women," *Shakespeare Jahrbuch* 134: 29–43.

Radin, Victoria (1987) "From Outer Space," *New Statesman*, 9 January.

Rich, Frank (1999) "Clinton Beats Dole (II)," *New York Times*, 23 January, A19.

Riggio, Milla Cozart (ed.) (1999) *Teaching Shakespeare through Performance*, New York: Modern Language Association.

Roach, Joseph (1985) *The Player's Passion: Studies in the Science of Acting*, Newark: University of Delaware Press.

Roberts, Jeanne Addison (1978) "'Wife' or 'Wise' – *The Tempest* l. 1786," *University of Virginia Studies in Bibliography* 31: 203–8.

Rodenburg, Patsy (1992) *The Right to Speak: Working with the Voice*, London: Methuen.

—— (1993) *The Need for Words: Voice and the Text*, London: Methuen.

—— (1997) *The Actor Speaks: Voice and the Performer*, London: Methuen.

Roszak, Theodore (1999) "Shakespeare Never Lost a Manuscript to a Computer Crash," *New York Times*, 11 March, G8.

Royal Shakespeare Company (1986) Program for *Heresies*, Stratford-upon-Avon.

—— (1987a) *111th Report of the Council*, Stratford-upon-Avon.

—— (1987b) *RSC Yearbook 1985/86, 1986/87*, Stratford-upon-Avon.

—— (1995) Program for *The Taming of the Shrew*, Stratford-upon-Avon.

Rutter, Carol (1989) *Clamorous Voices: Shakespeare's Women Today*, Faith Evans (ed.), London and New York: Routledge.

Salter, Denis (1996) "Acting Shakespeare in Postcolonial Space," in James C. Bulman (ed.), *Shakespeare, Theory, and Performance*, London and New York: Routledge, 113–32.

Schafer, Elizabeth (1998) *MsDirecting Shakespeare: Women Direct Shakespeare*, London: The Women's Press.

Shakespeare, William (1997) *The Norton Shakespeare: Based on the Oxford Edition*, Stephen Greenblatt, *et al.* (eds), New York and London: W. W. Norton & Co.

Shaughnessy, Robert (1994) *Representing Shakespeare: England, History and the RSC*, Hemel Hempstead: Harvester Wheatsheaf.

Shaw, Fiona (1995) Interview with the author, London, 5 September.

Shulman, Milton (1986) "Naive Feminist Notions," *Evening Standard*, 17 December.

Siberry, Michael (1998) "Petruccio," in Robert Smallwood (ed.), *Players of Shakespeare 4: Further Essays in Shakespearian Performance by Players with the Royal Shakespeare Company*, Cambridge: Cambridge University Press, 45–59.

Sinfield, Alan (1985) "Royal Shakespeare: Theatre and the Making of Ideology," in Jonathan Dollimore and Alan Sinfield (eds), *Political Shakespeare: New Essays in Cultural Materialism*, Ithaca, NY: Cornell University Press, 158–81.

—— (1991) *Faultlines: The Politics of Dissident Reading*, Berkeley: University of California Press.

—— (1994) "Heritage and the Market, Regulation and Desublimation," in Jonathan Dollimore and Alan Sinfield (eds), *Political Shakespeare: Essays in Cultural Materialism*, Second Edition, Ithaca and London: Cornell University Press, 255–80.

Spencer, Charles (1995) Review of *The Taming of the Shrew*, *Daily Telegraph*, 24 April.

Spevack, Marvin (1968) *A Complete and Systematic Concordance to the Works of Shakespeare*, Hildesheim: George Olms Verlagsbuchhandlung.

Staiger, Janet (1992) *Interpreting Films: Studies in the Historical Reception of American Cinema*, Princeton: Princeton University Press.

Starks, Lisa S. (1999) "The Displaced Body of Desire: Sexuality in Kenneth Branagh's *Hamlet*," in Christy Desmet and Robert Sawyer (eds), *Shakespeare and Appropriation*, London and New York: Routledge, 160–78.

Styan, J. L. (1977) *The Shakespeare Revolution: Criticism and Performance in the Twentieth Century*, Cambridge: Cambridge University Press.

Taylor, Gary (1989) *Reinventing Shakespeare: A Cultural History, from the Restoration to the Present*, New York: Oxford University Press.

—— (1999) "Theatrical Proximities: The Stratford Festival 1998," *Shakespeare Quarterly* 50: 334–54.

Taylor, Paul (1995) Review of *The Taming of the Shrew*, *Independent*, 24 April.

Thomas, Angela (1986) "Hand [*sic*] Up in Arms at RSC Women's Attack," *Stage and Television Today*, 10 April.

Thompson, Ann (ed.) (1984) *The Taming of the Shrew*, William Shakespeare, Cambridge: Cambridge University Press.

Tinker, Jack (1995) Review of *The Taming of the Shrew*, *Daily Mail*, 22 April.

Todd, Susan Lily (1995) Interview with the author, Totnes, Devon, 24 November.

Walter, Harriet (1993) "The Heroine, the Harpy, and the Human Being," *New Theatre Quarterly* 34: 110–20.

Wandor, Michelene (1986) *Carry On, Understudies: Theatre and Sexual Politics*, Revised edition, London and New York: Routledge and Kegan Paul.

Wardle, Irving (1995) Review of *The Taming of the Shrew*, *Independent on Sunday*, 30 April.

Weinraub, Bernard (1999) "Morning After Complaints Follow Miramax Mogul's Big Night," *New York Times*, 23 March.

Wells, Stanley and Gary Taylor (1987) *William Shakespeare: A Textual Companion*, with John Jowett and William Montgomery, Oxford: Oxford University Press.

Werner, Sarah (1996) "Performing Shakespeare: Voice Training and the Feminist Actor," *New Theatre Quarterly* 47: 249–58.

—— (1997) "Voice Training, Shakespeare, and Feminism (Reply to Cicely Berry, Patsy Rodenburg, and Kristin Linklater)," *New Theatre Quarterly* 50: 183.

—— (1998) "Notes on Sharing the Cake," in Lizbeth Goodman (ed.) with Jane de Gay, *The Routledge Reader in Gender and Performance*, London and New York: Routledge, 108–12.

Wilson, Edwin (ed.) (1961) *Shaw on Shakespeare: An Anthology of Bernard Shaw's Writings on the Plays and Productions of Shakespeare*, New York: E. P. Dutton & Co.

Wilson, John K. (1997) "Come Not to Bury Shakespeare: He Lives," *Chronicle of Higher Education*, 14 February, B6.

Wintour, Patrick and Stephen Bates (1993) "Major Goes Back to the Old Values," *Guardian*, 9 October, 6.

Woddis, Carole (1987) "A Woman's Role," *Plays and Players* 409: 14–16.

Worthen, W. B. (1997) *Shakespeare and the Authority of Performance*, Cambridge: Cambridge University Press.

Zeffirelli, Franco (1991) dir. *Hamlet*, with Mel Gibson and Glenn Close, Warner Bros.

Ziegler, Georgianna (1999) "Accommodating the Virago: Nineteenth-century Representations of Lady Macbeth," in Christy Desmet and Robert Sawyer (eds), *Shakespeare and Appropriation*, London and New York: Routledge, 117–41.

Index